# LEARNING FAMILY BUSINESS

*To our families:*
*Tricia, Anthea and Chris Moores,*
*Tom and Matthew Mylne*

# Learning Family Business

## Paradoxes and pathways

KEN MOORES
*Bond University, Australia*

MARY BARRETT
*Griffith University, Australia*

With commentary and cases from America's
foremost family business 'gurus': Leon and Katie Danco

# ASHGATE

Published by
Ashgate Publishing Limited
Gower House
Croft Road
Aldershot
Hampshire GU11 3HR
England

Ashgate Publishing Company
Suite 420
101 Cherry Street
Burlington, VT 05401-4405
USA

Ashgate website: http://www.ashgate.com

**British Library Cataloguing in Publication Data**
Moores, Ken
    Learning family business : paradoxes and pathways
    1.Family-owned business enterprises - Management
    I.Title II.Barrett, Mary
    658'.04

**Library of Congress Control Number**: 2002107423

ISBN 0 7546 0940 5

Printed and bound in Great Britain by Antony Rowe Ltd, Chippenham, Wiltshire

# Contents

# List of Figures

# List of Tables

# Preface

This book, like many other projects, grew from a starting point that was much smaller than the outcome might suggest. We have long been interested in what makes family businesses tick, the stages of their development and in how their CEOs had learned the skills to manage them and make them grow. And many family firms have indeed grown, often well beyond the vision of their founders and well beyond the category of 'small business' which is so often – and wrongly – brought to many people's minds when they hear the term 'family business'.

We have researched these issues in a variety of ways over the years, from mail surveys of senior managers in family firms to formal interviews with firm members to in-depth case studies of particular firms involving a multitude of measurements and other ways of scrutinizing firm and industry variables. Among all these approaches, we have given special weight to the ideas of family firm members themselves, many of whom have had considerable experience in businesses other than their own. In their efforts to compare their business with others we have heard one phrase recur dozens if not hundreds of times: 'It's just like any other business, except ...'. This phrase would invariably be followed by a description of something that marked family businesses as truly different from others, whether it involved the culture and values of the firm, how its leaders set goals for the firm and monitored progress towards them, how and where it was felt business experience was to be gained, how leadership succession was to be managed and a multitude of other things.

We are not the first to acknowledge that there are issues for family businesses that make them worthy of consideration as a special business category. In this book we have tried to explain the ways the 'different', even paradoxical, nature of family businesses affects how their aspiring leaders set out to learn how to manage them and the strategic choices they make in the process of trying to ensure their firms survive and grow. Along with Charles Handy who, in *The Empty Raincoat*, pointed out how all management is increasingly paradoxical, we have tried to see how recognizing and thus 'framing' the paradoxes of family business which appear at various stages of both learning family firms can help in exploring, understanding and, perhaps, *managing* them.

The term 'management' here is deliberately modest. We have not been in search of 'solutions' or 'quick fixes' to the paradoxes, since this would suggest that they can be made to disappear. Rather we have explored how the experiences of incumbent CEOs of family firms and the strategic choices they have made during the development of the firm, as evidenced by the stage the firm has reached in the business life cycle, provide some broad profiles and pathways consistent with family firm survival and growth.

It seems that family firms do indeed differ from non-family firms, but does this mean that, like Tolstoy's happy families, successful family firms are all alike? Since we neither sought nor ever expected to find any universal prescriptions for family firm success, we would have to answer no. But there seem to be at least some guiding patterns and principles that members, advisors, leaders and aspiring leaders of family firms, as well as business and management educators, will find useful. We hope that our efforts to explain them here will help all these parties in their efforts to understand and lead family firms to their full potential.

*Ken Moores and Mary Barrett*

# Acknowledgements

Many people have helped us with the research for this book and the preparation of the manuscript. We are indebted in particular to Leon and Katie Danco, for the time they gladly spent in our offices as we checked our ideas with them and gathered the fruits of their long experience consulting with family businesses. We thank Joe Mula, who participated in the original study upon which some of the findings are based. This study was sponsored by Horwath and Horwath Pty Ltd and we are grateful to them for their ongoing interest in the project and support for other family business activities in which we are involved.

For work in the course of the study itself, we are grateful to Vicki Wolyncevic who helped gather interview data and Diane Shao who transcribed the extended interview with Leon and Katie Danco. Justin Craig was tireless in retrieving previous research and made numerous useful suggestions for the improvement of the book as a whole. Tom Mylne was characteristically patient and careful in designing tables and diagrams and formatting the manuscript for publication.

The research for this book was assisted by a grant from the Australian Centre for Family Business at Bond University. We also thank the staff of the Centre for their practical support, especially for linking us with family business owners who were happy to be interviewed and otherwise participate in the research.

Our greatest thanks are reserved for owners and other members of many Australian family businesses whose ideas and experiences were invaluable for our research project, and who are the reason for the book's existence.

# Chapter 1

# Frameworks and Descriptions

It is strange that we don't know more about family owned business – how they are managed and how family members learn about the business. After all, this sector has been the backbone of most free enterprise economies and Australia has been no exception. In fact family businesses have been vital to the Australian economy since early colonial times. However when business is studied in most countries, it tends to be categorized and studied by researchers and government agencies alike in terms of size or industry segment. Curiously, attention to family owned business as a separate and important sector is all but ignored. Family business is usually lumped into the small business category. It is distinguished by virtue of its ownership being in the hands of a family group, and that's that. Well, perhaps there is more to the story.

To begin with, not all family businesses are small. Names like Packer, Smorgon, Murdoch, Fairfax, Fox, Pratt, Hancock, Kidman, Holmes à Court, Lowry and Myer have littered Australia's corporate scene for decades. Glance down the list of *Business Review Weekly*'s annual list of Australia's 'Top 500 profit earners' and you will get a feel for the significance of family owned business in Australia. A vast majority of those listed are still operating within what are essentially family business structures. Certainly most had their origins in a family business. Family owned businesses are represented in all segments within the private sector and across most industries. Many small family owned enterprises have been managed successfully through a series of transitions to become medium-sized, and even large enterprises. So what is it about these families and the conduct of their businesses which has enabled them to survive and grow? And what lessons can we learn from the study of family business in Australia?

Because of the economic significance of the family owned business in Australia, the sector warrants examination in its own right, separate from analysis of the small business sector. The success and longevity of many family businesses in Australia suggests they are doing something right. But what is it? To develop insight, the starting point must be to examine successful family owned businesses *and how their owners have learned to manage them.*

On the other side of the coin, many family businesses fail to survive beyond the first generation. Anecdotal evidence from the United States reported by America's guru of family business, Dr. Leon Danco, suggests that only 30 per cent of family businesses survive to the second generation, and a mere 13 per cent make it to the third generation and beyond. Reed (1989) estimates that the average life of family owned businesses in the United States is 24 years, which matches the average period of involvement of their founders. Do these unsuccessful firms differ in any systematic way from firms which make the transition to the next generation and beyond, and continue to survive and grow? And finally, are there any lessons in general which can be learned from successful family businesses which can be applied to the non-family business sector? Perhaps the 'family' is the critical factor for success.

The research we conducted for this book was undertaken in Australia. However, comparing our results with other research suggests our findings have a good deal to say about family businesses elsewhere. This is useful because, even internationally, research on family business is still an emerging field. Leon Danco, recognized by many as the founder of the field of family business consulting in the United States, began working in this area only in the early 1960s and wrote the first book based on his consultancy work in the mid 1970s. Formal academic research on family owned business gathered momentum in the United States around 1984 with the establishment of the Family Firms Institute, and its accompanying academic journal, *Family Business Review*. As Lansberg (1993, p. 316) points out, before the work of Barbara Hollander, the founder of the Family Firms Institute, there was little or no recognition that family business needed to be treated conceptually as a hyphenated term, that is, as more than 'a business with a family attached'.

The unique issues faced by family business operators in Australia led to the establishment of the Australian Centre for Family Business at Bond University, Queensland, Australia. Opened in 1994, the Centre's main goals are to undertake basic and applied research aimed at increasing the survival and success rates of family business; to collect, analyze and disseminate the results of local and overseas research with particular relevance to Australian business; and to support its affiliated national network, now known as Family Business Australia. A central focus of the Centre is the development of programs for family business owners and managers.

In this book we explain what we have learned from our research into how owners of successful family businesses learn to manage various transition phases in their businesses and in their own lives. In the case of family owned business the two are closely entwined. The research was complex, and we explain in detail how we went about it in the Appendix. Broadly speaking, however, using a combination of qualitative and quantitative techniques, we investigated how owners of a broad spectrum of family owned businesses in Australia learn business, learn to run *their* business, and learn how to *lead* their business, and finally, how they learn to *let go* that business. We also explored some of the pathways successful family owned businesses have found through the challenges presented by the business environment. After the opening chapters, which set the scene for family business in Australia and its impact both in that country and on the world economy, we explore each of these learning issues in turn. The themes that emerge for each stage of learning are surprisingly common across family businesses in general. Moreover, comparing the experiences of our family business owners with others elsewhere in the world reveals many similar themes. Thus our study, while preserving a distinctly Australian perspective, sheds light on the experiences of learning family business elsewhere in the world.

Of course, many similar issues are faced by all businesses, not just businesses that are family owned. But our research shows that in managing family owned businesses, some paradoxes appear that require special handling if the business is to be successful. Charles Handy, in *The Empty Raincoat* (1994), pointed out that the kinds of changes our society is undergoing have increasingly led to managers having to cope with paradox (p. 22). These paradoxes cannot be resolved and made to disappear – they can only be *managed*. Our research shows that running a family business also means dealing with paradoxes that defy ultimate resolution. Nevertheless, framing the paradoxes gives us a basis for beginning to understand and manage them. So our main task is to show what these paradoxes are for family businesses and how their owners have coped with them.

Before we begin to examine these paradoxes and how to manage them, however, it is helpful to understand what we mean by family owned business. Different views of what family businesses are also affect our understanding of their contribution to the economy both in Australia and elsewhere.

## Defining Family Business

In studies conducted in the United States, Britain and Canada over the last few decades, a number of working definitions for family businesses have been adopted. Family businesses have been variously defined in terms of their size, ownership and governance structures. Rosenblatt *et al.* (1985) define family business as 'majority ownership or control within a single family, and in which two or more family members are, or at some time were, directly involved in the business'. These aspects of ownership, control, and management were also evident in a frequently cited London Business School study for the accounting firm, Stoy Hayward. In that study, family businesses were defined as having any *one* of the following characteristics:

- more than 50 per cent of the voting shares owned by a single family;
- a single family group effectively controlling the firm; or
- a significant proportion of the firm's senior management from the same family.

As noted by Meredith (1988), the Canadian Association of Family Enterprises and the United States Family Firms Institute define a family business as one with the majority of key executive positions filled by members of the extended family, and (usually) the founder and spouse holding the majority of equity – children and other relations may find a place at key management levels. More recent United States studies tend to echo one or more of these definitional elements. Galiano and Vinturella (1995), for example, endorse the *Family Business Review* approach, which defines a family business as 'a business in which the members of a family have legal control over ownership' (p. 178). Ward and Aronoff (1996, p. 2) shift the emphasis somewhat, arguing that a family firm 'is one that includes two or more members of a family that has financial control of the company'.

These definitions of family business stress control by members of just one generation. Equally often, however, definitions follow the view proposed in the classic article by Donnelly (1964) on managing the strengths and weaknesses of a family business. Both strengths and weaknesses, in his view, stem from what a family business essentially is: 'a business [*which*] ... has been closely identified with *at least two* generations of a family and [*where*] this link has had a mutual influence on company policy and on the interests and the objectives of the family' (p. 93, our italics). However while many commentators and researchers insist either implicitly or explicitly that members of more than one generation need to be represented in the business for the 'future-oriented' nature of family business to become apparent, Shanker and Astrachan (1996) note that others take the opposite tack, arguing that even businesses run by only one person should be considered family businesses because of the contribution of other family members and the impact of the business on them.

Still other researchers such as Wortmann (1994) have bemoaned the lack of a 'unifying conceptual framework' for the study of family business. It is debatable whether a single paradigm for the study of family business is possible or even desirable. However there have certainly been attempts to meet Wortmann's challenge, and some of these are relevant to the issue of defining family business. An example is Litz (1995) who combines the distinction between ownership and management set out by Berle and Means in 1934 with the notion of 'intraorganizational aspirations'. With this term Litz tries to capture an 'intention-based' definition of family business which would allow researchers to examine movement towards the family firm or, conversely, the possibility of family firms becoming non-family businesses either deliberately or by default.

**Towards an Australian Definition of Family Business**

The Australian Bureau of Statistics (ABS) provides the closest to an official Australian definition of family business in its 1990 definition of small business. The ABS defines small business as being independently owned and operated, and closely controlled by the owners/managers, who also contribute most, if not all, the operating capital, and who make the principal operating and financial decisions. The ABS acknowledges the difficulty of using this definition for statistical data collection purposes, and circumvents the problem by using numbers of employees to define small business. So when the ABS collects data, a small business is defined as one which employs fewer than 20 persons in non-manufacturing industries and fewer than 100 persons in manufacturing industry. More recently, in *A Portrait of Australian Business: Results of the 1995 Business Longitudinal Survey*, published jointly by the Industry Commission and the Department of Industry, Science and Tourism (DIST), the operational difficulties and the lack of validity of a definition of a business form based simply on size were acknowledged. This publication acknowledges three main elements of a family business:

- succession (defined as the ownership of the business by a successor of a previous owner);
- employment of family (so that family members who may not have any management involvement are employed by the business); and
- shared managerial responsibilities (so that family members are jointly responsible for the running of the business).

However, in the first year of the *Business Longitudinal Survey*, the third aspect of the definition seemed to be the most important, since data had been gathered on businesses where there was more than one proprietor from the same family. For future Australian family business research a definition based on the key features of family, ownership (control), and business is more appropriate than one which emphasizes only one of these factors. To this end the following points may help us develop a definition for family owned business research:

- *Family*: The 'family' means a group related by blood or marriage, including siblings, spouses and children. More than one family can be involved in the business and they may not be related.
- *Ownership (control)*: The family must have the capacity to effectively control the financial and operating decisions of the business. The most generally accepted defining characteristics of control include ownership within the family or families of a substantial share of the equity; the ability to control the board, trustees or partners; or family members located in key senior management positions. Some studies of American family businesses have vested control in the family with as little as five per cent of the shares. Furthermore, a case could be made for a family having control when only one family member sits on the company's board of directors. This is most likely the case when the board is chaired by a strong founder who has sufficient control purely by the force of his or her personality, rather than necessarily by a controlling shareholding.
- *Business*: The ABS focuses on the business unit or enterprise rather than any legal or divisional structures of the business. Families can operate a number of legal structures as separate businesses. If this occurs, then the concept sought is of a family's control of the group of businesses or the whole enterprise.

The *Business Longitudinal Survey* puts this ABS definition into practice by collecting data on 'the management unit' – that is, the highest level accounting unit within a business operating in a given industry for which detailed accounts are maintained. While in nearly all cases it coincides with the legal entity owning the business, that is, a company, partnership, trust or sole operator, it is acknowledged that large diversified businesses may have more than one management unit, each coinciding with a 'division' or a 'line of business'. The ABS collects data on each of these lines of business so long as 'separate and comprehensive accounts' are available (ABS, 1990, p. 3).

Bearing these points in mind, a workable definition of family business developed for our research is as follows:

> A grouping of persons related by blood or marriage (the family) who control a business enterprise through ownership, or who possess the capacity to control the governing body of the business. The enterprise may be comprised of one or more legal entities as defined by the ABS (1990).

## Size and Significance of Family Business

Defining family business is important not merely because researchers want to be able to compare findings, but because variations of definition affect an understanding of the contribution of family business to national economies. The significance of family owned corporations occurs not only through their ownership and control of private corporations but also their impact through public corporations. In their authoritative study of corporate ownership around the world, La Porta, Lopez-de-Salanes and Shleifer (1999), cited in Schulze *et al.* (2001), found that family members participate in the management of at least 69 per cent of firms they control. (Control is defined as 10 per cent ownership.) Moreover, families on average control 35 per cent of the largest firms in the richest countries in the world, compared to the 24 per cent that are widely held, and the 20 per cent that are controlled by the state. Family control becomes more prevalent as firm size falls, with families controlling approximately 53 per cent of the world's medium-sized firms ($500 million in revenues), compared to the 20 per cent that are state controlled and the 11 per cent that are widely held. Various other groups account for the remainder.

The importance of family management varies greatly around the world. In the United States and Canada, families control about 30 per cent of the largest public firms and directly participate in the management in about a third of them (*Forbes*, 2000; Kang, 2000). While families control only about 10 per cent of the largest firms in Australia, Japan, Finland and Germany, they control 50 per cent of the largest firms in Belgium and Israel, 55 per cent in Sweden, 65 per cent in Argentina and Greece, 70 per cent in Hong Kong and 100 per cent in Mexico (La Porta, Lopez-de-Salanes and Shleifer, 1999).

However influential the role of families is through these public corporations, their contribution has been more widely acknowledged through the private entities they own and control. In the United Kingdom the family owned business sector is the largest employer group, while in the United States its significance is indicated by the following frequently cited statistics:

- more than 98 per cent of the 14 million businesses registered in the United States are privately owned, and more than 90 per cent are family businesses (Beckhard and Dyer, 1983);
- among US *Fortune* magazine's top 500 companies, more than one third are family controlled (Reed, 1989);
- family owned businesses produce half the United States' gross national product and employ half the nation's workforce (Timmons, 1990).

These and other statistics have been criticized by Shanker and Astrachan (1996) on the grounds that they have been so frequently cited that their primary sources cannot be located. For these authors, many of the claims made about the significance of family businesses' economic contribution come from 'street lore' rather than solid empirical research. They suggest, for example, that we should distinguish between broad, middle and narrow definitions of family business. A broad definition would include businesses where no family member is in direct daily contact with the business but still has influence over the decisions made, perhaps by sitting on the board or owning a significant percentage of the equity. The middle division would include all the criteria of the broadest group, as well as requiring that the founder or descendant(s) of the founder run the company. The narrowest family business definition would require that the business have multiple generations involved, direct family involvement in daily operations, and more than one family member having significant management responsibility (Shanker and Astrachan, 1996, p. 122). More stringent, empirically based research relying on narrower definitions of family business, suggests a smaller, but still very important economic contribution of family business to the economy.

**Table 1.1   Contribution of family business to the United States economy**

| | Broad definition of family business | Narrow definition of family business |
|---|---|---|
| Total number of family businesses in the US | 20,332,400 | 4,121,300 |
| Family business contribution to US GDP | 49% | 12% |
| Percentage of total US workforce | 59% | 15% |
| Family business contribution to job creation 1988-1990 | 78% | 19% |

*Source*: Adapted from Shanker and Astrachan (1996).

The significance of these variations in the definition of family business is clear from a comparison of the columns in Table 1.1. While a narrow definition of family business means a smaller economic contribution from this sector, its importance remains clear. As a result, the ways family businesses are run are being recognized as providing an exemplary focus for businesses in general. For example, the requirement in the United States that public corporations report quarterly encourages a short-term focus, whereas family owned businesses, among many other advantages, appear to take a longer term perspective to investment and to be more durable during recession (Brokow, 1992; Aronoff and Ward, 1995). Intention-based definitions of family business, that is, definitions which stress the intention of family business owners to retain long term control of the business within the family reinforce this point. Baring (1992) found CEOs of family businesses held the position for more than 15 years, and an additional 35 per cent held the position between seven and 14 years. By contrast, commentators often point to the short-term focus of public corporations as being responsible for the loss of America's competitive position in world markets.

Less is known about the size, composition, importance, and success and failure factors of family owned businesses in Australia. What knowledge we have suggests the significance of the sector is similar to that in the US and the UK. Australia's economy is made up of many industrial sectors. A significant sector that cuts across many industries is the small business sector. McMahon (1986) reports that over 90 per cent of Australian businesses are small; more recently the Australian Bureau of Statistics (1997) estimated that 95 per cent of business enterprises are small. However, the small business failure rate is high, with two-thirds of all such businesses beginning to fail within their first five years of operation (Small Business Development Corporation, 1990). The major reasons for failure include liquidity problems, lack of management experience and capabilities, and poor records and information systems.

Family-owned and operated businesses make up a major subgroup of the small business sector. Clearly, family businesses being managed and operated by second, third, and later generations have been successful in surviving beyond the initial five years of operation. It is worth noting, however, that whereas many Australian small businesses are indeed family owned and operated, not all family firms are small. Many have been successfully managed through a series of transitions to become medium in size and even large enterprises contributing significantly to the Australian economy.

As mentioned earlier, the ABS has until recently only collected data based on firm size and type of industry. However the *Business Longitudinal Survey* which, every five years, collects data based on the number of proprietors from the same family, now provides a basic indicator of the contribution of family business to the Australian economy. The survey results are based on 6,000 businesses and extrapolations are made from this to the rest of the family business sector.

The study suggests that, of Australian firms across all industries and excluding those with only one proprietor, 50.8 per cent have some or all proprietors from the same family (Industry Commission and Department of Industry, Science and Technology (DIST), 1997, p. 53). The same survey also suggests that 75.4 per cent of all firms employing more than 100 people have some or all proprietors from the same family (Industry Commission and Department of Industry, Science and Technology (DIST), 1997, p. 51). These figures suggest that there is much to be gained from looking at success factors in larger family owned businesses in Australia as well as smaller ones, and the manner in which these larger firms have endured and grown.

Our book aims to do just that, or at least to begin the task. While we might guess that much of what overseas researchers have said might apply to Australian family owned businesses we cannot be sure without doing our own research. This book discusses the issues involved in learning and managing Australian family owned businesses. It also brings some systematic insights into the view often expressed by owners of family business that 'it's just like any other business, except ...'. But when we say systematic, we don't mean simple or easy! On the contrary, the phrase 'it's just like any other business, except ...' usually pointed to the need to recognize and live with paradoxes. These paradoxes arise from the priorities that are associated with the distinct stages in learning the family business: Learning business, Learning *our* business, Learning to *lead* our business and Learning to *let go* our business. Rather than making the paradoxes disappear, the business owners we spoke to had found pathways through them. These priorities, paradoxes and pathways are the true subject of our book.

## References

Australian Bureau of Statistics (1990), *Small Business in Australia 1990*, Catalogue 1320.0. Canberra, Australian Bureau of Statistics.

Australian Bureau of Statistics (1997), *A Portrait of Australian Business*, DIST Publication Number 007/97, Canberra, Australian Bureau of Statistics.

*Forbes*. (2000), 'Are dynasties dying?' (editorial), vol. 165, no. 6, pp. 126-31.

Galiano, Alanna M. and Vinturella, John B. (1995), 'Implications of Gender Bias in the Family Business', *Family Business Review*, vol. 8, no. 3, pp. 177-88.

Handy, Charles (1994), *The Empty Raincoat*, London, Random House.

Industry Commission and Department of Industry, Science and Tourism (DIST) (1997), *A Portrait of Australian Business: Results of the 1995 Business Longitudinal Survey*, Canberra, Australian Government Publishing Service.

Kang, D. (2000), 'The impact of family ownership on performance in public organizations: A Study of the U.S. Fortune 500, 1982-1994', Presentation at the 2000 Academy of Management Meetings, Toronto, Canada.

Lansberg, I. (1993), 'Reflections of the Founder: A Conversation with Barbara Hollander', *Family Business Review*, vol. 6, no. 3, pp. 313-25.

La Porta, R., Lopez-de-Salanes, F., Shleifer, A. (1999), 'Corporate ownership around the world', *Journal of Finance*, vol. 54, no. 2, pp. 471-517.

Litz, Reginald A. (1995), 'The Family Business: Toward Definitional Clarity', *Family Business Review*, vol. 8, no. 2, pp. 71-82.

McMahon, R. G. P. (1986), *Financial Management for Small Business*. North Ryde, CCH Australia.

Meredith, G. (1988), 'The Family in Business – A Neglected Area of Research', *Management Forum*, vol. 14, no. 1, pp. 63-4.

Reed, N. (1989), 'Make it, Milk it, Lose it', *The Australian Accountant*, March.

Rosenblatt, P. C., de Mik, L., Anderson, R. M. and Johnson, P. A. (1985), *The Family Business*, San Francisco, Jossey-Bass.

Schulze, William S., Lubatkin, Michael H., Dino, Richard N. and Buchholtz, Ann K. (2001), 'Agency Relationships in Family Firms: Theory and Evidence', *Organization Science*, vol. 12, no. 2, March-April, pp. 99-116.

Shanker, Melissa Carey and Astrachan, Joseph H. (1996), 'Myths and Realities: Family Businesses' Contribution to the US Economy', in *Family Business: Gateway to the Future: Proceedings of the 1995 Family Firm Institute Conference October 11-14*, St. Louis, MO, Family Firm Institute, pp. 120-39.

Small Business Development Corporation (1990), *A Study of the Profiles of Inexperienced Small Business Operators and the Case for Management Training*, Brisbane, Small Business Development Corporation.

Stoy Hayward (1989), *Managing Family Business in the UK*, Monograph, London, Stoy Hayward.

Timmons, J. A. (1990), *New Venture Creation: Entrepreneurship in the 1990s*, Homewood, Irwin.

Ward, John L. and Aronoff, Craig E. (1990), 'Just What Is A Family Business?', *Nation's Business*, U.S. Chamber of Commerce, February.

Wortmann, Max S. (1994), 'Theoretical Foundations for Family-Owned Business: A Conceptual and Research-Based Paradigm', *Family Business Review*, vol. 7, no. 1, pp. 3-28.

# Chapter 2

# Learning, Life Cycles and Love: A Contingency Perspective on Family Business

## The Business Context: Sources of Uncertainty

All firms face uncertainties. The origins of these uncertainties are both internal and external to the firm. In the case of family firms, these uncertainties can emanate from the stages of family, ownership and business development. As Gersick *et al.* (1999) point out, some of the most critical and challenging moments in the development of family enterprises are linked to the internal changes between ownership and family stages. They have examined how family enterprises manage the internal transitions associated with ownership development. They acknowledge family and business development, but concentrate on ownership issues. Our focus, by contrast, is primarily on the external uncertainties emerging during business development, although we acknowledge family and ownership development issues.

Accordingly, for us, external uncertainties are evident in questions such as: Are technology levels changing rapidly? Is the firm's industry dynamic and risky? Are the tastes and preferences of customers changing? Is public opinion changing? Could the government make changes which will affect the firm? How are general economic conditions going to affect the firm? The origins of internal uncertainties are often related to the firm's structure, giving rise to questions such as: How should work and management in the firm be organized as the firm grows? How should ownership of the firm be structured as the needs of proprietors change?

These internal and external uncertainties are sometimes referred to as contingencies. Taken together, they add up to the firm's *context*. Given the context, a firm – whether family owned or not – needs to engineer its internal situation to best fit its external environment. Some of the uncertainties (or contingencies) most often seen as affecting firms' ways of attempting to fit their environment include environmental uncertainty, task uncertainty, production technology, shared organizational knowledge of goals and throughput mechanisms, and organization size. These factors and others have a long history of research and investigation by organizational theorists.

Uncertainties arising from these factors lead to differences in how managers try to lead their firms, that is, how they set goals for their firms and monitor progress towards these goals. Yet there are broad consistencies in the approaches managers can be seen to apply. One way of discussing firms' various approaches to coping with uncertainty is to see the approaches as *strategies*. While the individual effects of and firm reactions to factors such as markets, technology, customer tastes and preferences, and so on have been subjected to separate study, they have also been found to cluster together to define types. These include strategy types such as the Defender, Prospector, Analyzer and Reactor framework defined by Miles and Snow (1978).

But there are other ways of looking at the issue. A particularly useful approach to understanding the kinds of clusters, or organizational configurations, of these factors is to see them as being associated with firm developmental stages such as the *organizational life cycle*. Let us take a moment to consider in more detail this approach to both implementing and understanding firms' approaches to dealing with the uncertainties of their environment.

## The Organizational Life Cycle

All organizations change over time. Some make these changes rapidly in revolutionary modes whereas others bring about change through evolutionary modes (Miller, 1992). These changes manifest themselves in different organizational strategies, structures, or processes and have been refereed to as transitions (Kimberly and Quinn, 1984). Such transitions often occur in response to external demands of opportunities such as changes in the economy, competitor behaviour, capital or labour markets, or government regulations.

Changes in the internal state of a firm also prompt transitions As an organization moves from start up to steady state or enters a period of growth or retrenchment, significant alterations may be required in the aspirations of the firm or in its internal structures and systems (Hackman, 1984). Life cycle theory implies that organizations go through states that both follow predictable patterns and are not easily reversed (see, for example, Quinn and Cameron, 1983; Kimberly, Miles and Associates,

1980; Kimberly and Quinn, 1984). To make these transitional changes successfully requires careful management that knows the underlying dynamics of the system. Part of that management includes the use of 'appropriate' internal structures and systems to exercise control. There are various ways in which management can seek to control these organizational stages and transitions, ranging from informal mechanisms to highly sophisticated formal systems.

The organizational life cycle is a good framework for understanding the uncertainties in the business environment and how organizations cope with them since, as theorists and practitioners alike have found, there are no universal principles which will guarantee firm survival and success. By the firm's life cycle we mean a set of changes that follow a predictable set of developmental stages. These stages occur in a hierarchical progression that is not easily reversed, and involve a broad range of organizational activities and structures.

As Quinn and Cameron (1983) point out, various authors who have written on the topic have emphasized specific sets of organizational characteristics in their models of the organizational life cycle. We will only look at one model in detail, the one developed by Adizes (1979), because it best accounts for both maturing and declining stages of the life cycle.

*Adizes' Managerial Roles*

Adizes' life cycle model describes four broad managerial roles. A well managed organization must *P*roduce results, it must be *A*dministered, it must adapt through *E*ntrepreneurial creativity, and it must be *I*ntegrated.

*Producing* refers to being effective, ensuring organizational goals are met. Ideally, this should occur in an efficient manner and requires an *Administration system* which helps managers to make the right decisions at the right time. Creativity and risk-taking, associated with the *Entrepreneurial role*, are important for long term survival as firms must be able to adapt to their changing environment. Similarly, *Integrating* the firm and building a cohesive team are important to getting things done and a long life-span.

At different stages in an organization's life there will be a different mix and emphasis on these four roles. Getting this mix right is management's main task. If this role selection is mismanaged, the business may not survive and prosper. The four letters (*PAEI*) represent the four key roles, *P*roduce results, *A*dministration, *E*ntrepreneurial creativity, and *I*ntegration. The capitalized letter represents the role(s) which should be dominant in order for the firm to be successful. In addition to this changing mix of managerial roles, the management system of the firm will vary with the life cycle stage. Differing mixes of management techniques will be associated with each growth stage of successful firms.

Adizes identified ten distinct stages in the life of a typical business. These range from the courtship through to the death stage and include infancy, go-go, adolescence, prime, mature, aristocratic, and early and full bureaucratic stages. Figure 2.1 on pp. 18-19 summarizes the dominant management approaches and cultures of each life cycle stage. In addition, it points out the dangers for out-of-control organizations.

*Adizes' Ten Stages of the Organizational Life Cycle*

Adizes identifies ten distinct stages within the organizational life cycle. Together with the typical variations in the associated Production, Administration, Entrepreneurship and Integration roles, they can be described as follows:

*Courtship*  In the initial **courtship** stage (roles = *paEi*), the emphasis is on entrepreneuring. A sense of excitement and missionary zeal imposing a formal management system could be counterproductive. Typically, there are minimal financial or human resources to support any systems. Nevertheless, financial simulations may prove useful in assessing various scenarios that the founders identify. It is important for CEOs whose firms are in the 'courtship' stage of their development to draw on an advisory group consisting of their lawyers, accountants, friends and business contacts to provide a sounding panel of expertise and impartiality crucial for developing a well rounded and potentially successful idea. Many ideas may be aborted at this stage because they are not seen to be viable.

*The infant organization*  It is crucial for the **infant** organization (roles = *Paei*) to produce results. Typically, there will be virtually no systems, procedures or policies in an infant organization. This is partly because the organization cannot afford them, but also because formal systems would not facilitate reactions fast enough to deal with the constant decision problems faced by a young, growing firm. Furthermore, many of the decisions will be unique and outside the control parameters of most 'normal' systems.

A fledgling firm's mistakes in marketing, design or financial planning are likely to result in infant mortality. This is because such firms lack managerial depth, experience or a track record. Avoiding such crises by minimizing the risks of the operation in the early stages improves a firm's chances of success. McNamara and Moores (1988) found that adopting a risk reduction strategy was the key difference between a sample of successful and unsuccessful (failed) new ventures. The types of risks controlled for, and the relevant management strategies adopted are summarized in Table 2.1. McNamara and Moores also found that using formal systems and accounting based controls was limited in both successful and unsuccessful firms in their early stages of development. We can tentatively conclude from their work that an overall risk reduction strategy, rather than any specific control system whether formal or informal, will be most beneficial for infant organizations.

**Table 2.1    Risks and successful strategies in young firms**

| Type of risk | Successful management strategy |
| --- | --- |
| Viability of the market | Market research |
| Product risks | Produce substitute products and conduct product trials |
| Market penetration | Produce quality product cheaper |
| Lack of innovation | Hire quality personnel |
| General uncertainties | Produce a portfolio of products |

*Source*: McNamara and Moores (1988).

*The 'go-go' organization*    In the **go-go** stage (roles = *PaEi*), the organization is still very results orientated but now has 'time to think'. When go-go firms 'think' about risk reducing strategies they are effectively applying broad management controls that forestall the installation of formal systems. A strong directive board to converge the 'go-go' thinking and to improve sloppy 'back of an envelope' planning will help these risk reduction strategies to be adopted. However the need for formal management systems continues to grow and is merely deferred by the use of such strategies. In stable environments statutory and tax reporting considerations will emerge as the dominant features of the management system. However, in the more likely turbulent environment of the small, growing firm, accounting controls such as monthly profit and loss and balance sheet accounts, ratio analysis and flexible budgets will more effectively facilitate control.

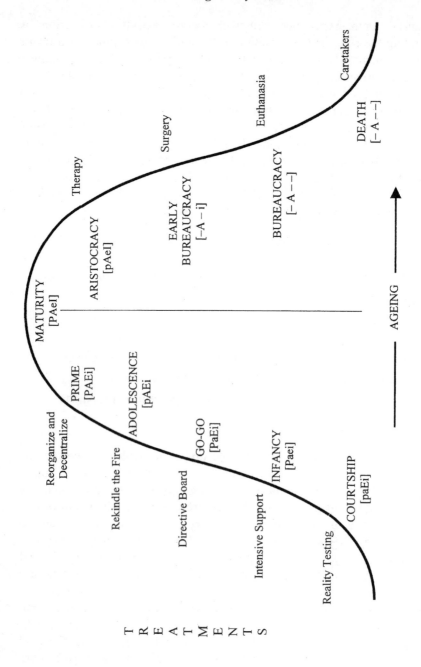

**Figure 2.1    The stages of the organizational life cycle**

**Characteristics of Ascending Firms**

* 'E' dominates the organizational culture
* Control ethos: everything permitted unless specifically forbidden
* Function dominates form
* Political power with marketing and sales
* Necessary to facilitate convergent thinking
* Internal agents of change

**TREATMENT: PREVENTATIVE**

**Characteristics of Descending Firms**

* 'A' dominates the organizational culture
* Control ethos: everything forbidden unless specifically permitted
* Form dominates function
* Political power with finance and accounting
* Necessary to facilitate divergent thinking
* External agents of change

**TREATMENT: CURATIVE**

**Figure 2.1 (continued)**

*Source*: Adapted from Adizes (1979) and Moores (1990).

*The adolescent organization* The **adolescent** organization (roles = *pAEi*) is typified by an increasing administrative role. Administration through a system of output controls enables operational decision-making to be delegated. According to Child (1984), output controls depend on measuring output variables for management purposes and are desirable for adolescent firms as they avoid the costs and demotivating aspects of either close personal supervision or a fully fledged bureaucratic control system. A responsibility based accounting system is the most suitable output control for adolescent firms and should initially incorporate elements of actual costing and cashflow analysis.

As the adolescent firm grows in size the output controls which dominate the control system for small firms will give way to an administrative system, incorporating increasing levels of bureaucratic controls. A bureaucratic control strategy involves the three Ss of scientific management: *specialization* which leads to *simplification*, and thus enables *standardization*. Child (1984) says that the accounting control systems most compatible with such a control strategy are budgetary controls and standard costing. Other accounting control techniques that prove useful in the **adolescent** organization include flexible budgets, industry analysis, and break-even analysis.

*The prime organization* The **prime** organization (roles = *PAEi*) has an entrepreneurial orientation and is productive. It also has an administrative system that efficiently plans and deals with decision problems and has streamlined procedures. Research on new ventures and new products (Cooper, 1979; Cooper and Bruno, 1977; Maidique, 1983; Maidique and Roure, 1985; McNamara and Moores, 1988; Myers and Marquis, 1969; Rothwell *et al.*, 1974; Rubenstein *et al.*, 1976; Van de Ven, Hudson and Schroeder, 1984) suggests that the exact nature of an organization's management system will depend on the degree of environmental turbulence the firm faces and the structural complexity of the organization. Firms that are approaching the prime stage will tend to be larger and will tend to have more complex organizational structures in place partly to cope with size and partly to 'get the job done'. More mature firms will tend to have a greater range of products and will require functional specialization (e.g. marketing, finance, production) as well functional interaction. As a result firm structure later in the life cycle will be more complex.

*The mature organization*  The decline of the entrepreneurial role in the prime stage is replaced by a focus on integration. This change signifies the **maturing** of the organization (roles = *PAeI*). The climate in a mature organization is more formal. Systems begin to dominate the firm. Eventually, the results orientation is affected as there is no longer an eagerness to excel because the firm is out of touch with the market's needs. The decline from maturity can be slow or fast and depends on the nature of the industry in which the organization is located. With no entrepreneurial input, high technology firms can die very quickly. The final four stages in Adizes' (1979) model cover this decline phase. Part of the problem during these stages is that organizations are over controlled by inappropriate systems.

*The aristocratic organization*  In the **aristocratic** organization (roles = *pAeI*), it is not what you do and why you do it that are important, but how you do it. Tradition rather than performance is emphasized. Essentially management by history dominates. Creativity and risk-taking associated with entrepreneurship is not entertained. Integration to achieve a uniform behaviour pattern is the message.

*Early and fully bureaucratic organizations*  The next two stages reflect increasing levels of bureaucracy. Firstly, **early bureaucracy** (roles = –*A*–*i*) is characterized by an emphasis on personal survival. 'Knowing how to work the system' is the only way to get things done. However, when organizations are in **full bureaucracy** stage (roles = –*A*– –), nothing really gets done because teamwork is all but absent. Only systems, rules and procedures persist. Some areas of the public service are familiar examples of this stage of decline. The motto in such organizations is 'put it in writing'. Adizes (1979, p. 13) describes this stage thus:

> In full-blown Bureaucracy very little, if anything, gets done. There is no fighting: there is an atmosphere of peacefulness. Such organizations' managers are among the nicest to work with. They agree a lot. But nothing ever happens.

*Death*  At **death**, there are no roles!  The organization ceases operations and is liquidated.

## A Summary View of the Organizational Life Cycle

Quinn and Cameron (1983) looked at nine different life cycle models which had been developed at the time. They observed that these models had a common element: they progressed through similar developmental stages. Accordingly, Quinn and Cameron (1983) synthesized this diverse literature and described a four-stage summary model to accommodate the nine models. Their summary model suggests organizations progress through an *entrepreneurial stage*, a *collectivity stage*, a *formalization and control stage*, and a *structure elaboration stage*.

During the *Entrepreneurial stage* ideas are marshalled, entrepreneurial activities occur but with little planning and coordination. The business positions itself in a 'niche', and if a 'prime mover' advantage exists, a certain amount of power is conferred. The *Collectivity* stage is characterized by an atmosphere of collectivity, where a sense of mission pervades activities with high levels of commitment. Communication and structure are informal. During this stage innovation continues to occur. The business then passes into the *Formalization and control* stage. By now rules have been formalized and the structure stabilized. Essentially, the stage can be described as conservative, with institutionalized procedures. After a time, the business progresses into a renewal phase, known as the *Elaboration of structure* stage. The business becomes decentralized and its domain is expanded as it learns to adapt to new challenges.

Quinn and Cameron (1983) integrated Adizes' model into their summary model by suggesting the parallels outlined in Table 2.2 below. According to Quinn and Cameron (1983), Adizes (1979) does not include the fourth stage, elaboration of structure. But in our opinion, a careful reading of Adizes (1979) suggests that certain Prime and Mature organizations adopt decentralized structures as a means of organizational renewal and adaptation. As such, elaboration of structure is contemplated in the Adizes (1979) model at or about prime and maturity stages.

## The Business Life Cycle – A Contingency View of Firm Management

The lesson of the life cycle ideas propounded by Adizes (1979) and others is that the stage of the business life cycle has a profound effect on the priorities of managing firms. So understanding the business life cycle stage is an important aid to the thinking of managers about how to manage their firms in relation to elements of the external and internal environment.

**Table 2.2    Comparison of life cycle models**

| Adizes Model | | Summary Model | |
|---|---|---|---|
| 1 Courtship | | Stage 1 | Entrepreneurial |
| 2 Infancy | } | Stage 2 | Collectivity |
| 3 Go-Go | | | |
| 4 Adolescence | | Stage 3 | Formalization and Control |
| 5 Prime | } | Stage 4 | Formalization and Control/ Elaboration of Structure |
| 6 Maturity | | | |
| 7 Aristocracy | } | *Declining stages are not covered by the Summary Model* | |
| 8 Early Bureaucracy | | | |
| 9 Bureaucracy | | | |
| 10 Death | | | |

These days, this 'contingency' approach to management is familiar to us, at least at a broad level. That is, we are accustomed to seeing organizational effectiveness not simply as a result of finding the 'one best way' of managing, but rather as a product of an appropriate matching between internal organizational characteristics and the demands of various elements of context such as technology and the external environment. The contingency perspective has not always held sway, however, and there is still a strong temptation to rely on the approaches of the early days of management thinking, when Fayol and others discussed universal approaches to management functions such as planning, organizing, coordinating and controlling. In the research which contributes to this book, we made considerable use of contingency perspectives, particularly in terms of the ways various forms of firm activity are linked to the business life cycle. In particular we investigated the extent to which the business life cycle stage moderates firms' responses to specific aspects of their environment. We focussed on family owned businesses that are being managed by second (or later) generation family members since they represent sites that have already undergone the early transitions represented in Adizes' life cycle stages. Figure 2.2 shows the theoretical framework of our research investigation.

As we will see over the next five chapters, the business life cycle is also helpful for illuminating the stages of learning the family business. For now, however, let us look more closely at some of the sources of uncertainty we mentioned at the beginning of this chapter as making up the firm's context.

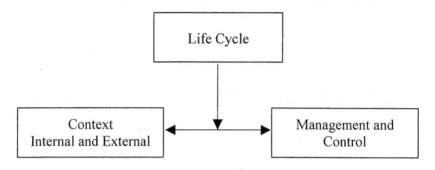

**Figure 2.2      Theoretical framework**

*Environmental Uncertainty*

External environmental uncertainty has long been recognized as an influential variable in contingency-based theories of organization design (see, for example, Burns and Stalker, 1961; Thompson, 1967). Previous research, such as studies carried out by Gordon and Narayanan (1984) and Chenhall and Morris (1986), has also linked environmental uncertainty to the type of information – especially accounting information – that managers perceive to be useful. That is, managers seek out different kinds of information depending on whether the external environment is turbulent (e.g. highly competitive, changing rapidly) or not. Govindarajan (1984) tried to find a more explicit interaction approach relating uncertainty, managers' use of information, and firm performance. He considered the impact of environmental uncertainty and managers' style of evaluation on the performance of strategic business units (SBUs). He found no relationship between managers' evaluative style and the performance of their SBUs. However, it was clear that managers facing high uncertainty were likely to be evaluated in a more subjective manner than were managers facing lower uncertainty. In addition, he found that whether there was a consistent relationship between SBU effectiveness and managers' evaluative styles depended on the extent of external uncertainty. Similarly, Brownell (1985, 1987) found that, in situations of low environmental uncertainty, firm performance was improved if managers put a high emphasis on meeting budgets.

## Task Uncertainty

In contrast to the various contingencies which constitute the firm's external environment, task uncertainty – or the degree to which a required task is closed or open-ended – is an aspect of a firm's internal environment. It has also been the focus of studies into firm effectiveness. For example, Hirst (1981) concluded that relying on accounting performance measures under conditions of task uncertainty does not help firms to be effective. Instead, he suggested that what employees working in the firm thought and did was more important. Specifically, he argued that staff would adjust their perceptions and behaviour according to the level of task uncertainty they were exposed to, and also the extent to which their boss relied on accounting performance measures in evaluating them. His contingency-style conclusion was that having the boss rely to a medium to high extent on accounting performance measures when doing staff evaluations would lead to the most effective behaviours in situations of *low* task uncertainty. However in situations of high task uncertainty, employees are most effective if their bosses rely much *less* on accounting performance measures when evaluating their staff. These results are, of course, not directly comparable with those of Govindarajan and Brownell, but they do suggest that performance evaluation systems should rely less on formal accounting controls in uncertain conditions.

## Technology

A variety of studies have identified associations between different dimensions of technology and characteristics of how firms develop their control systems. For example, Daft and Macintosh (1984) found a link between the nature of technical processes (job, batch, process) with the amount, focus and style of data that managers collect to measure firm performance. Merchant (1984) identified an association between the degree of automation and how formally budgets were used. Merchant (1985) linked the predictability of production processes with budgetary slack. Chenhall and Morris (1986) found that interdependence within production processes was associated with the characteristics of information managers perceived to be useful. Macintosh and Daft (1987) found an association between departmental interdependence and a low dependence on standard operating procedures, budgets and statistical reports.

While these studies draw on very different notions of technology, the results indicate that dimensions of technology affect the design of control systems in terms of the relative ease of control. Complex, non-programmable, automated or interdependent processes do not seem to fit well with conventional control systems such as budgets and standard operating procedures. Relying on conventional control systems too heavily in these situations may even lead to dysfunctional behaviours.

*Organizational Structure*

Organizational structure is concerned with formally specifying different roles for organizational members, or tasks for groups, to ensure that the activities of the organization are carried out. Large and technically sophisticated firms have been found to favour decentralization and structuring with a strong emphasis on control systems. By contrast, small and dependent firms were more likely to be centralized and to reduce managers' autonomy (Bruns and Waterhouse, 1975). Merchant (1984) found that differentiating parts of firms by their functions, for example, finance, sales, production, and so on, was associated with developing more formal budgets. Gordon and Naranayan (1984) found organic structures were linked with managers gathering and using future orientated information. Chenhall and Morris (1986) found that the extent to which a firm was decentralized made a difference to how useful managers found aggregated and integrated information. Again, while these studies are not strictly comparable, there seem to be some common themes in their conclusions. Organizations with high levels of formal decentralization or mechanistic structure arrangements use more formal and comprehensive control systems. However, factors such as environment, technology and size can influence this relationship.

**Dealing With Uncertainty**

In the preceding discussion, we mentioned some of the responses to specific types of uncertainty that organizations produce in an attempt to meet their objectives. Control can be thought of as a process of guiding a set of variables to attain a preconceived goal or objective. Thus in an organizational sense, control refers to attempts by managers or other stakeholders within an organization to influence the behaviour and activities of company personnel to achieve desired outcomes (Moores and Mula, 2000). Thus firms' responses can be thought of as *controls*. The importance of control is also reflected in the prominence of this issue in definitions of family firms. When we examined the various definitions of family firms, we touched on just a few approaches to establishing controls but many others are possible. As a result of the variety of approaches, there is also a huge quantity of research about control, but no dominant approach to how the research should be undertaken (Merchant and Simons, 1986). This makes research studies in the control area difficult to compare, contrast, and integrate. In an effort to understand the complexities of control, various ways of classifying it have been suggested (Anthony, 1988; Child, 1984; Hopwood, 1974; Jaworski, 1988; Merchant, 1985; Ouchi, 1979). It is useful at this point to examine some of the best known of these classification approaches, to then to see what they have in common.

Hopwood (1974) described the pattern of organizational control as consisting of administrative, social, and self controls. *Administrative* controls are the formal rules and procedures found in most organizations. *Social* controls emerge from the values and commitments shared by all members of the organization. *Self* or *personal* controls are those which the individual exerts over his or her own behaviour.

Ouchi (1979) divides his control framework into market, bureaucratic, and clan controls. These are pure forms of control, which will not be found in organizations, which contain some features of each. *Market*-based controls operate through a system of prices established in arm's length transactions, and no artificial administrative control system is necessary to produce the required information as the price mechanism is itself the control mechanism. Where firms have instead internalized many transactional exchanges through a system of transfer of prices, control is achieved by various *bureaucratic* rules and procedures. *Clan* controls provide great regularity of relations and may, in fact, be more directive than the other mechanisms. Clan controls may employ a system of legitimate authority, but they are more often based on traditions rather than rational/legal forms. Clan controls are exercised through a common socialization into the corporate culture readily accepting its values and beliefs. Our research and that of others suggests that clan controls may be especially important in family businesses.

Child (1984) developed four significant strategies of control in organizations, namely personal centralized, bureaucratic, output, and cultural controls. *Personal centralized* control is a form of control that is dependent on a key person for supervision and reward, usually the owner of the firm. *Bureaucratic* controls depend on formal procedures with tasks being broken into easily definable elements. *Output* controls link rewards to attainable and measurable outputs. *Cultural* control provides an environment where there are few formal controls as there is goal congruence between individuals and the organization.

Merchant (1985) identifies three categories of control: results, action, and personnel controls. *Results* controls reside in formal accounting systems and are represented by such accounting performance measures as net income, return on investment, earnings per share. *Action* controls take the form of constraints on behaviour, pre-action reviews and action accountability. *Personnel* controls revolve around the interaction of people in groups and the managerial actions that motivate and influence their behaviour.

*Common Views of Control*

Some common views of control emerge from these broad approaches as well as other studies of how control mechanisms in firms work in practice. They include a need for balance and consistency in control mechanisms, as well as the observation that certain types of controls seem to cluster together.

*Balance of controls* Although each of our four classification approaches uses different terminology, all researchers agree that formal controls need to coexist with non-formal controls. As early as the fifties, Anthony (1952, p. 47) suggested that 'management control is most effective when the formal and informal techniques are skilfully blended'. In support of the general proposition of the importance of non-financial controls, Brownell (1987) notes that financial information constitutes only a part of one group of controls available to organizations. Brownell adds that accounting-based controls represent just the 'tip of the iceberg' when it comes to considering all possible controls available to organizations.

*Consistency of controls* Additionally, many researchers point out that all forms of controls must be internally consistent and must be considered together in the organizational context in which they are being applied.

## The Family – An Additional Factor

Family firms are no less affected by environmental uncertainty and the other sources of uncertainty we discussed earlier. Their development and management control approaches can equally well be defined in terms of the their position on the business life cycle and in terms of the formal and informal approaches outlined by Hopwood, Ouchi and others. However a family business must also contend with the *family*.

The relationship between the family and the business is a crucial characteristic of the family owned business. As we will see, the values and beliefs commonly shared by family members introduce a strong cultural dimension that often conflicts with purely rational economic demands. These broader family values and beliefs provide meaning to the way family members relate to their business. Accordingly, management systems within family firms must accommodate the impact that such cultures can have on the effectiveness of various management strategies.

We pointed out earlier the frequent finding in research on control that there should be consistency both between the control approaches themselves, and between the control approaches and the firm's external and internal environment. The values that characterize family business form part of the demand for control consistency that researchers have seen. Merchant (1985), for example, argues that there should be consistency between the intent and structure of management systems and firm values, particularly when controls are part of more comprehensive systems and processes. Put simply, major decisions in the family firm will affect both the family and the business systems. The family business establishes sets of values, norms and principles that generate behaviour which is adapted to the needs of both the family and business (Davis and Stern, 1980). The challenge is to maintain appropriate boundaries between the family and the tasks required for the successful development and operation of the business. External factors and family issues must be accommodated simultaneously for the firm to survive and grow (Beckhard and Dyer, 1983).

The interdependency between ownership and management creates forces which make executive and strategic decisions more complex and more subjective. These complex relationships are summed up in the ways many business owners talk about managing a family business as, on the one hand, 'just like any other business' and, on the other hand, fundamentally different. This is indicated by the tendency of family business owners to follow the description of their business as 'just like any other business' with the word 'except ...'. They then proceed to describe something to suggest that family businesses are very *unlike* other businesses.

The coexistence of ownership, management and corporate interests is illustrated in Figure 2.3 overleaf.

*Learning Family Business*

## Publicly Owned Corporation

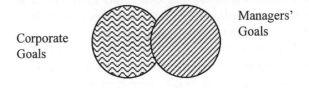

Corporate
Goals

Managers'
Goals

## Family Owned Business
### Shared Goals

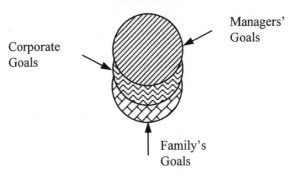

Corporate
Goals

Managers'
Goals

Family's
Goals

## Family Owned Business
### Divergent Goals

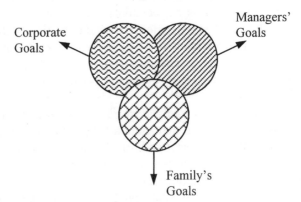

Corporate
Goals

Managers'
Goals

Family's
Goals

**Figure 2.3      Relationships and goals in family business**

*Source*: Giles, 1992.

This figure makes it clear how introducing the element of the family suddenly makes the whole management problem of family businesses both more simple and more complex. On the one hand, the problem of managing a family business becomes more simple because there is potential for managers' and corporate goals to converge because of the family link. However, there is also more potential for the goals to diverge and conflict, which creates additional complexities and paradoxes in managing a family business.

The problem, of course, is to know in what circumstances goal convergence and goal divergence are likely to appear. Agency theory deals with the issues surrounding agency costs, that is, the costs incurred in creating management and control systems to ensure that managers' decisions are kept in line with owners' interests and do not result in expropriation of shareholder wealth through consumption of perquisites and the misallocation of resources (Fama and Jensen, 1983a, p. 332). Schulze *et al.* (2001, pp. 99-100) and Fama and Jensen (1983b, p. 306) point out that according to Jensen's and Meckling's model of agency costs (called hereafter the J/M model), there are three reasons why family firms, at least those that are privately held and family-managed, could be expected not to incur such costs. First, the alignment of interests of owners and managers in family firms reduces managers' incentives to be opportunistic. Second, property rights in family firms are largely restricted to 'internal decision agents' whose personal involvement ensures that managers will not divert shareholder wealth to their own, separate purposes. Finally, the J/M model predicts that family management will mean shares tend to be held by '... agents whose special relations with other decision agents allow agency problems to be controlled without separation of the management and control decisions. Family members [...] therefore have advantages in monitoring and disciplining related decision agents'.

The J/M model is intuitively appealing, and it seems to provide a rationale for the finding of many researchers that clan controls are especially important in family firms. Yet the empirical work of Schulze *et al.* (2001) has not borne out the model's predictions. These researchers, using data from one of the largest surveys of American family businesses ever undertaken, tested a series of hypotheses derived from the concept that family firms should incur fewer agency costs. They found that virtually all the hypotheses consistent with the J/M model were unsupported. Specifically, they found that in family firms the payment of incentives to non-family agents, the use of strategic planning, the disclosure of the major shareholder's estate and share transfer intentions and good governance practices, all characterized firms that performed *better* than family firms which did not have these characteristics. The J/M model would predict that these measures are unnecessary, and likely even to be counterproductive. The only hypothesis consistent with the J/M model that was not shown to be dubious was the payment of incentives to family agents. This practice was not found to be positively related to the performance of privately held, family managed firms.

As a result of their findings Schulze *et al.* (2001) argue that, contrary to the idea that family firms necessarily represent one of the least costly (most efficient) forms of organizational governance (Daily and Dollinger, 1992; Kang, 2000), private ownership and family management expose firms to agency hazards. These hazards arise for a variety of reasons. As Schulze *et al.* (2001, p. 100) explain, private ownership frees family firms from the discipline imposed by the market for corporate control and increases the agency threat posed by self-control. Family firms also face adverse selection due to the effect of private ownership on the efficiency of their labour markets. Finally, altruism alters the incentive structure of family managed firms in ways that offset many of the agency benefits, such as commitment, gained through family management. They conclude that a positive relationship exists between agency costs incurred by family firms and their performance.

Yet how are we – and owners of family firms – to know the point where 'family' influences cease to be the source of goal convergence in family firms, as the J/M model predicts, and instead become the source of goal divergence, as the work of Schulze *et al.* shows they may well be? Our work suggests that the organizational life cycle, in framing the *progress* in the kinds of control measures family firms implement as they develop, helps to provide an answer to this question. At the same time, the organizational life cycle provides a framework for a series of learning tasks the aspiring leader of the family business needs to master.

## *Effect of Family on Business Learning*

Just as the element of 'family' in family owned businesses influences how they are managed, that is, how the manager deals with the contextual factors such as life cycle stage, context and control, the element of 'family' can be expected to influence how people in family owned businesses *learn* to manage them. In fact, having to deal with the additional layer of complexity created by the family means that the tasks and priorities involved in learning to manage a family business lead to specific and enduring paradoxes. The family will turn out to be just as important a contingency factor as any of the others in the business context – and often more so. And just as understanding the stage of the business life cycle helps illuminate management priorities in general, it can help in understanding the paradoxes that come with each stage of learning the family business.

## The Organization of This Book

But all this is to jump ahead in our story. The stages of learning, their particular paradoxes and even the pathways business owners have found to manage these paradoxes need to be understood more slowly. For this reason we have devoted a separate chapter to each stage of learning. So, from here, the book proceeds as follows. In Chapter 3 we examine the first stage of learning, which is simply 'Learning Business'. Here the stage of the business life cycle seems to do relatively little to illuminate the learning priorities for someone learning to manage a family business; the paradox of this stage and the pathways through it seem to be virtually universal. In the second learning stage, discussed in Chapter 4, we see how aspiring leaders have to learn about '*Our* Business', that is, how to understand and value the special qualities associated with, and indeed created by, the fact that it is a *family* business. The stage of the business life cycle the firm occupies will be seen to bring out some of the salient features of this phase of learning.

In the third stage, dealt with in Chapter 5, we consider what it is like to learn to '*Lead* our Business'. Leadership is a complex task in any firm, but there are some particularly tricky leadership issues for family firms. At this stage the business life cycle is a dominant learning tool in illuminating both what needs to be done and how it must be learnt. In Chapter 6, we consider the complexities of learning to '*Let Go* our Business'. Letting go is the task of leadership viewed from a different perspective – that of the person leaving the CEO position rather than the person assuming that role. As a result, the value of understanding the stage of the business life cycle is equally great in showing how this stage needs to be learned and managed.

Does this mean that we think things become impossible to understand – hopelessly paradoxical, perhaps – as firms progress along the life cycle curve to maturity, and as leaders learn to take on the complex task of managing them? Fortunately, things are not so tough. While the paradoxes of learning remain, our research into the experience of family business managers shows that there are patterns of firm survival and growth that recur. Again, understanding the stage the firm has reached on the business life cycle is a good way of understanding these patterns. The patterns do not form blueprints for success, but at least they offer some consistent guidance derived from the experience of managing successful family firms. Chapter 7, 'Profiles and Patterns that Work', sets out some of these patterns. Finally, for the technically minded, the Appendix provides a wealth of technical detail about the quantitative and qualitative approaches we used in our study of Australian family business.

### *Learning From Those Who Have Been There*

In each of the four 'Learning' chapters, we hear frequently from managers of family owned businesses who explain in their own words how they have discovered and dealt with the paradoxes of each learning stage. In addition, the wisdom and long experience of US family business consultants Leon and Katie Danco shows the broad-reaching nature of some of these issues. Their views together with the comments and insights of our business informants reveal that, at a certain level of abstraction, these issues are, if not universal, then certainly wider than one country. What their comments and our analyses show is that managing and learning family business is full of paradoxes. In the next chapter, 'Learning Business' we see the first of these paradoxes emerge.

### References

Adizes, I. (1979), 'Organizational Passages: Diagnosing and Treating Lifecycle Problems of Organizations', *Organizational Dynamics*, vol. 8, no. 1, pp. 2-25.
Anthony, R. N. (1952), *Management Controls in Industrial Research Organizations*, Cambridge, MA: Division of Research, Graduate School of Business, Harvard University Press.
Beckhard, R. and Dyer, W. G. Jr. (1983), 'FMR Forum: Managing Change In The Family Firm: Issues And Strategies', *Sloan Management Review*, Spring, pp. 59-66.
Brownell, P. (1985), 'Budgetary Systems and the Control of Functionally Differentiated Organizational Activities', *Journal of Accounting Research*, pp. 502-12.
Brownell, P. (1987), 'The Role of Accounting Information, Environment and Management Control in Multinational Organisations', *Accounting and Finance*, pp. 1-16.
Bruns, W. J. and Waterhouse, J. H. (1975), 'Budgetary control and organizational structure', *Journal of Accounting Research*, Autumn, pp. 177-203.
Burns, W. J. and Stalker, J. H. (1979), *The Management of Innovation*, London, Tavistock.
Chenhall, R. H. and Morris, D. (1986), 'The Impact of Structure, Environment and Interdependence on the Perceived Usefulness of Management Accounting Systems', *The Accounting Review*, vol. 61, no. 1, pp. 16-35.

Child, J. (1984), *Organization: A Guide to Problems and Practice*, London, Harper and Row.

Cooper, A. C. (1979), 'Identifying Industrial New Product Success: Project New-Prod', *Industrial Marketing Management*, vol. 8, no. 2, pp. 124-35.

Cooper, A. C. and Bruno, A. V. (1977), 'Success Among High-Technology Firms', *Business Horizons*, vol. 20, no. 2, pp. 16-22.

Daft, R. L. and Macintosh, N. B. (1984), 'A New Approach to the Design and Use of Management information', *California Management Review*, pp. 82-92.

Daily, C. M. and Dollinger, M. J. (1992), 'An empirical examination of ownership structure in family and professionally-managed firms', *Family Business Review*, vol. 5, no. 2, pp. 117-36.

Davis, P. and Stern, D. (1980), 'Adaptation, Survival and Growth of the Family Business: An Integrated Systems Perspective', *Human Relations*, vol. 34, no. 4, pp. 107-24.

Fama, E. and Jensen, M. C. (1983a), 'Agency problems and residual claims', *Journal of Law and Economics*, vol. 26, pp. 325-44.

Fama, E. and Jensen, M. C. (1983b), 'Separation of ownership and control', *Journal of Law and Economics*, vol. 26, pp. 301-25.

Galbraith, J. (1973), *Designing Complex Organizations*, Reading, Addison-Wesley.

Gersick, Kelin E., Lansberg, Ivan, Desjardins, Michele and Dunn, Barbara (1999), 'Stages and Transitions: Managing Change in the Family Business', *Family Business Review*, vol. 12, no. 4, December, pp. 287-97.

Giles, J. (1992), *Family and Business Controls in Family Owned Business: Case Study*, unpublished MAcc Project, Gold Coast, Bond University.

Gordon, L. A. and Narayanan, V. K. (1984), 'Management accounting systems, perceived environmental uncertainty and organization structure: An empirical investigation', *Accounting, Organizations and Society*, vol. 1, pp. 33-47.

Govindarajan, V. (1984), 'Appropriateness of Accounting Data in Performance Evaluation: An Empirical Examination of Environmental Uncertainty as an Intervening Variable', *Accounting, Organizations and Society*, pp. 125-35.

Hackman, J. R. (1984), 'The transition that hasn't happened', in J. R. Kimberly and R. E. Quinn (eds), *Managing Organizational Transitions*, Homewood, Il., Richard D. Irwin Inc.

Hirst, M. K. (1981), 'Accounting Information and the Evaluation of Subordinate Performance: A Situational Approach', *The Accounting Review*, pp. 771-84.

Hopwood, A. (1974), *Accounting and Human Behaviour*, London, Haymarket Publishing.

Jaworski, B. J. (1988), 'Towards a theory of marketing controls: Environmental context, control types, and consequences', *Journal of Marketing*, vol. 52, pp. 23-39.

Jensen, M. C. and Meckling, W. H. (1976), 'Theory of the firm: Managerial behavior, agency costs, and ownership structure', *Journal of Financial Economics*, vol. 3, pp. 305-60.

Kang, D. (2000), *The impact of family ownership on performance in public organizations: A study of the U.S. Fortune 500, 1982-1994*, 2000 Academy of Management Meetings, Toronto, Canada.

Kimberly, R. J., Miles, R. H. and Associates (1980), *The Organizational Life Cycle: Issues in the Criterion, Transformation, and Decline of Organizations*, San Francisco: Jossey-Bass.

Kimberly, R. J. and Quinn, R. E. (eds) (1984), *Managing Organizational Transitions*, Homewood, Il., Richard D. Irwin Inc.

Macintosh, N. B. and Daft, R. L. (1987), 'Management Control Systems and Departmental Interdependencies: An Empirical Study', *Accounting, Organizations and Society*, pp. 49-61.

Maidique, M. A. (1983), 'The Stanford Innovation Project: A Comparative Study of Success and Failure in High-technology Product Innovation', in *Proceedings of the Conference on Management of Technology Innovation*, National Science Foundation and Worcester Polytechnic Institute, Washington, DC.

Maidique, M. A. and Roure, J. B. (1985), *Key Factors in the Success and Failure of New Technological Ventures*, Working Paper, Stanford University.

McNamara, R. and Moores, K. (1988), *The Control of New Ventures: Risks, Strategies and Systems*, paper presented at the Australian and New Zealand Association of Management Educators' Conference, Perth.

Merchant, K. A. (1981), 'The design of the corporate budgeting system: Influences on managerial behavior and performance', *The Accounting Review*, October, pp. 813-29.

Merchant, K. A. (1984), 'Influences on departmental budgeting: An empirical examination of contingency models', *Accounting Review*, pp. 291-307.

Merchant, K. A. (1985), *Control of Business Organizations*, Marshfield, Pitman.

Merchant, K. A. and Simons, R. (1986), 'Research and control in complex organizations: An overview', *Journal of Accounting Literature*, pp. 183-203.

Miles, R. E. and Snow, C. C. (1978), *Organizational Strategy, Structure and Process*, New York, McGraw-Hill.

Miller, D. (1992), 'Environmental fit versus internal fit', *Organizational Science*, vol. 3, no. 3, pp. 159-78.

Moores, K. (1990), 'Control, culture and cycles: The changing role of accounting controls in successfully growing businesses', *Bond Management Review*, vol. 1, no. 1, pp. 63-75.

Moores, K. and Mula, J. (2000), 'The Salience of Market, Bureaucratic, and Clan Controls in the Management of Family firm Transitions: Some Tentative Australian Evidence', *Family Business Review*, vol. 13, no. 2, pp. 91-106.

Myers, L. and Marquis, D. G. (1969), *Successful Industrial Innovations*, National Science Foundation Report NSF 69-17.

Ouchi, W. G. (1979), 'A conceptual framework for the design of organizational control mechanisms', *Management Science*, September, pp. 833-48.

Quinn, R. E. and Cameron, K. (1983), 'Organizational life cycles and shifting criteria of effectiveness: Some preliminary evidence', *Management Science*, vol. 29, no. 1, pp. 33-51.

Rothwell, R., Freeman, C., Horsley, A., Jervis, V., Robertson, A. B. and Townsend, J. (1974), 'SAPPHO Updated – Project SAPPHO, Phase II', *Research Policy*, vol. 3, pp. 258-91.

Rubenstein, A. H., Chakrabarti, A. K., O'Keefe, R. D., Souder, W. E. and Young, H. C. (1976), 'Factors influencing Innovation Success at the Project Level', *Research Management*, vol. 19, May, pp. 15-20.

Schulze, William S., Lubatkin, Michael H., Dino, Richard N. and Buchholtz, Ann K. (2001), 'Agency Relationships in Family Firms: Theory and Evidence', *Organizational Science*, vol. 12, no. 2, March-April, pp. 99-116.

Thompson, J. D. (1967), *Organizations in Action*, New York, McGraw-Hill.

Van de Ven, A. H., Hudson, R. and Schroeder, D. M. (1984), 'Designing New Business Start Ups: Entrepreneurial, Organizational and Ecological Considerations', *Journal of Management*, vol. 10, no. 1, pp. 87-107.

# Chapter 3

# Learning Business

All CEOs need to learn the skills of managing a business. So we might assume many of these skills are common to all businesses, whatever their form of ownership. But what about family owned businesses? Are there issues for the family firm that mean you need to go beyond knowing what stage the firm has reached in its organizational life cycle? Do you need to learn things that are in some way special or different in order to manage your family-owned business? And do you need to learn them differently from how you would do this in a business that is not family owned?

Our research suggests the answer to all these questions is yes. It seems that, in addition to the skills needed to run any business, there are some special attitudes and skills needed to run a family owned business, and some special ways these attitudes and skills are acquired. In line with Donnelly's (1964) definition, and in order that we would be examining businesses which had survived the early stages of their development, the informants in our sample of family businesses were second-generation or later members of their enterprises. Most of them had had more formal education than their parents. Many, but by no means all, of the family business owners in our study expected in turn that their children would gain more educational qualifications than they had obtained, including business or other qualifications from colleges of technical and further education or university. It is vital, according to our informants, that this formal business training is sought outside the family business.

## Business is Undergraduate Study

Leon Danco endorses the need for a broad-based formal education for future business owners, and not necessarily in business. He points to the isolation that business people who have not had the time to devote to tertiary education endure. As he puts it:

> **Leon Danco**: The universities have a real place in broadening the mind to learn. Often learning, book learning, is not high on the list of business people's priorities because there is nobody to get the jobs done to give them the comfort of learning. So I think [*the problem*] is the spiral of people with minimum

education passing on the minimum education to their children. The business is becoming more complex than the independent, solitary, unadvised, undirected, unrevealed individual is going to handle. He will make one bad mistake and the firm goes.

In his view, the need for formal education is greatest among some of the immigrant communities from which independent-minded business people in the United States and Australia have traditionally come. While the personal courage of the immigrant encourages their spirit of self-reliance, in the end it is also liable to restrict their ability to handle their businesses in the longer term:

> **Leon Danco**: To a lot of people, there is no need to go beyond some minimum sixteen or seventeen year-old education, God knows what it is, particularly in rural areas. And I am amazed at the lack of what I call an 'intellectual life' in Australia. Some of these things are characteristics I see as an American, looking at a similar immigrant society. Whether we're from America or Australia, we are all children of immigrants who came at one point or another to this country. Think of the early immigrants' situation. They do not have anyone to turn to, they can't speak the language. In the States, you get a lot of people who don't speak English. You get a lot of people. And so they cluster together, they talk only with their own kind, and they become very independent. They call that pride: self-pride and so on. The boys say that if you don't take care of yourself, nobody else will. I would say that the Australians are the most independent of English-speaking people I've met. So when they get old, they don't take advice very easily. And they are not intellectual. They are physical. They are physical in every aspect.

In the course of our research, we noticed that our informants stressed the positive side of getting a formal education, and the need to leave home and the family business to do this. They didn't tend to enlarge on the negative consequences of not doing so. Perhaps this was because they had virtually all taken this path. Both Katie and Leon Danco, however, were quick to point out the negative effects of failing to push children out of the family business 'nest' in the interests of gaining a formal tertiary education. According to Katie Danco, mothers in family owned businesses sometimes encourage their children not to pursue university or other forms of tertiary education or employment elsewhere than in the family business. Instead, they encourage their children to enter the family business. When the mothers succeed in this, the children often enter the family business too early. The mother often does this because she has endured lonely times in the early years of the business, and wants to prevent her children and grandchildren moving too far away from her:

> **Katie Danco**: The reason [*is*] mother who has hardly seen anything of her husband. Her children have been starting to run away and go off, the mother of an eighteen year-old is likely to be forty, forty-five, fifty. ... It depends on whether there were multiple children. And dad is doing real well and life is comfortable, and she would like her grandchildren to be around her nest. And more mothers than not look upon the business as the milk for the cow and all her grandchildren are going to be around her. She says, 'My God, if little Johnny leaves Brisbane and goes to Perth, or leaves Sydney and goes to Brisbane, he will marry some girl he meets up there and they will go move away and I will never see my grandchildren'. I can cite you chapter and verse on that. So they say, 'Don't let the child find a job elsewhere. He's going to find a mate elsewhere and will move away and leave us'. And then everything she's worked for will disappear. Her grandchildren are going to be born and raised out of her sight.

According to both Katie and Leon Danco, the mother is a central figure in the family business, perhaps even more than the father. Because of the strength of the mother's influence on her children's attitudes, and whether or not she knows it, the mother in the family business may well determine whether the children learn to learn to value or reject the whole idea of being in business for themselves, let alone running the family business. It is up to her to bear in mind the effect of her views on the long-term future of the business:

> **Leon Danco**: I think it's a fact that the supportive wife is an absolute ingredient. Whether it is a supportive wife in the first generation, the second generation, the third generation, she can set the atmosphere. It is like not smoking. Children who are seven years old tell you that smoking is bad for you - where do they learn that? They've learnt it somewhere and you can't change their opinions. So she [*a supportive wife*] is setting in the kids' minds the idea that what daddy does is good and wonderful and great for the society and we are so proud of our daddy. He works very hard to do it because nothing comes free. But if you are good enough to work in daddy's business, that would be wonderful. That creates a mind that wants to make a contribution rather than seek an entitlement, or thinks that the business is the family cow to provide milk to kids at the lowest cost.

**Learning Priority: Proficiency**

From the experience of our informants as well as from Leon and Katie Danco, it was clear that the most important skills future business owners need to learn outside are *general* skills. Let us take a moment to see which of these skills are the most important.

*Self-Management Skills*

Foremost among the skills our informants mentioned were skills that relate to future business owners' ability to manage *themselves*. Interestingly, we found as we probed our informants that they placed more emphasis on acquiring specific attitudes and personal qualities and less on business skills. These attitudes and qualities included personal discipline and a sense of pride and self-reliance.

> Above all, what I learned in those early days is that it's pretty well up to me how things turn out. This doesn't mean I think I can do anything, but that if something's got to happen, it's going to need me to see it through.

> I found you never stop thinking about the business really. I can be out somewhere, having a good time, and something will occur to me, something I can use later. I've learnt not to resent that, even when it seems like an interruption. It's just the subconscious ticking over. I regard it as part of a habit of alertness and observation that you have to cultivate as part of your personal business discipline.

> What being in another business taught me was attention to detail. You can't afford just to gloss over those small things. It's one thing to look at 'the big picture' and of course you've got to be able to do that. But it's just as important to really know your business from the inside and to be prepared to look at small things that might indicate something is not going as well as it should.

*People Skills*

After self-management skills, our informants typically mentioned a range of other general skills; of which the one most often nominated first was 'people skills'. One of our informants who ran a motor dealership franchise as a family business put this among the most important skills of the many her son had to acquire outside the business. As she said of his experience when she sent him to work in a different franchise located in a different state:

He then had to feel the brunt of his staff, getting the best out of his people, doing deals, keeping within budgets, buying cars, etc. ... And the point was, he found he couldn't do it all by himself. He knew a lot – or thought he did. What he really had to learn was how to produce the results by getting people to work as a team. It only took one person not to follow up and the deal was lost. He had to learn not to blame that person, but to blame himself for not making sure they knew what they had to do. ...

However for many family business owners, 'people skills' had a broader meaning than simply learning how to get on with people, get the best from people's creativity, learn how to network, or even how to work with a team. Family business owners typically linked a wide range of *general learning* issues to people skills – often in ways we did not expect. For them, 'people skills' are part valuing practical knowledge over theory. People skills are also connected to family business owners' commitment to ongoing learning and research, and, as part of this, their efforts to make best use of their own and other people's creativity. Let us look at these issues in turn and how each of them was first learned outside the family business.

*Practical Knowledge*

In general, family business owners, like business owners in general, valued practical knowledge over theoretical knowledge. From the manager of a market research and consulting firm:

> In the consulting industry in general, I believe there is a need to develop the practical and the creative abilities of people. Our universities are still training people too much in analysis and theory at the expense of creativity and practice. They need to remember that, in business, 'money flows towards great ideas, well executed'.

> [...]

> That was what I first learned from working in other businesses before I was seriously considered as a potential manager of this firm. The people I most respected in those firms I worked in earlier hadn't necessarily spent a lot of time poring over books. They'd had an idea – a good one – and just pushed ahead with it. Sometimes against a lot of opposition.

*Ongoing Learning*

Family business owners regularly stressed the importance of ongoing learning in all areas of the business:

> We are constantly trying to search for better ways through feasibility and cost studies as well as documented processes and training. We also look at other businesses doing the same thing. I've never been knocked back when I've asked to visit them [*other businesses*] and have them show me how they've employed a particular strategy. Likely future developments are always being considered. We're also looking for better ways to communicate to clients.

Again, the informant stressed that this was something that had first impressed him when he saw other firms doing it:

> That's something you've got to be convinced about early on. If you only see your own family business, which might be pretty stable by the time you are really taking notice of how it's run, you mightn't realize how hungry your competitors are. It's easy to get a bit too comfortable! But I never was really in danger of doing that because I worked in places where someone was always out researching something in the marketplace, even if it was just how well or badly they'd gone with the last idea.

An investment in formal research is part of this continuous learning process. From the owner of an industrial design firm:

> We invest a lot in research, mainly through travelling to see what others are doing here and overseas. We are also inspired by client requests to find an innovative way to do something different. For example, if they [*the clients*] are metal workers we might try to make their design work look like it's got rivets in it, or we might even put rivets into it. Use research – extensive research – within what the market allows. Be prepared to engage with some risk – trial and error. Trial new ideas.

This CEO urges that others be prepared to engage in risk-taking, but his advice can also be read as a recommendation to scan the firm's external environment as a form of risk reduction or uncertainty avoidance. Ongoing learning in the form of looking outside the firm becomes a form of anticipatory control. He puts some of his continual 'scanning' activity down to his own inherent restlessness and interest in doing things better. However he also credits some of his focus on research to some early outside experience. As he said during another part of the interview:

It's funny when you think about it, but the part I liked best about working there was what they called the 'playroom'. That was what they called the area of the production site where they devised and tested out new products. Everyone was encouraged to go and look at what was being tried out this week or this month. … It didn't matter that you weren't working on the production side. If you had something useful to say about it – or even if you just took a careful interest – they'd listen. They said some of their best ideas came from just listening to people coming through. …

## People Skills and Creativity

Another informant, a caterer, stressed the importance of understanding the relationship between his personality and the creativity of his people:

Being a power freak and terribly right brain, it [*innovation*] generally comes from me. I've been very fortunate with the people I've had working closely with me. I can say, 'Here's an idea. What can you do with it?'. And we can compromise and come up with something brilliant.

[…]

The boss in the firm I first worked for knew how important it was to share ideas. People in this business can be cagey with their ideas now. And it's got worse in restaurants – chefs are like film stars all too often. But back then, he encouraged us to share – by giving us his own best ideas to develop and then giving us the credit. Those were good times.

Learning from the rest of the business team is important. As one business owner says about the sources of his ideas:

It's usually me [*who comes up with new ideas*] but we encourage others to contribute. My management team co-ordinates all new ideas and tests them out. People get the credit.

[…]

I learnt early that no one person's idea is enough. I worked for my uncle in the early days, and he would always say that he couldn't ever remember where some of the good ideas had come from. He wasn't just being modest. The rest of us knew the basis of an innovation was generally something that had come from him. But he knew how important it was to take an idea and build on it. He used to point out how far a product had developed and changed from how he first envisaged it, and how much better other people had made it.

So ideas are only the beginning. Involving a range of other people is valuable in the all-important stage of assessing an idea for its feasibility and the likelihood it will add value to the business. From a clothing retailer:

> If an idea comes up and I like it, I put it to our management staff. We judge it on whether it makes business more profitable, helps our systems, customers, ease of implementation – these things decide whether it is implemented or not.

But making those decisions can be tough. It can be difficult both to encourage people to be creative and to pick the ideas that will really fly. From a partner in a law firm:

> The first question I ask is, 'How will it work?'. It might seem like an obvious question but it is not always to the one bringing the idea forward. If it seems to 'have legs', we trial it. It's got to be practical and the bottom line able to be demonstrated. If they don't have the commitment to follow through I don't see why I should take up the running on it. However, if they do, I'll back them one hundred per cent.

In his view this habit of careful inquiry and calculated risk were part of his early, outside training for business:

> I spent time in other law firms, of course and even then I liked to poke my nose in and see how the whole show was run, not just what happened in particular cases. I was young and impatient and I was always coming up with what I thought was a better way of doing what they had spent years doing. But the senior partners never told me to get lost. One of them always said, 'Give me just two reasons why I should do this'. He was saying 'two' to give me the idea that he was interested – I didn't even have to find three reasons. Of course, when he asked me more questions about my two reasons, I found I had to come up with solid evidence, just like any other part of legal work. He wouldn't change things just to indulge me.

## Other Skills

Beyond personal management and the broad range of people skills, our informants typically emphasized the technical skills of business as important and best learnt outside. Finance and accounting skills were seen as among the most important of the skills needed for general business proficiency. However the value of other skills such as selling, knowing the current market, having the ability to pick where the market would go, were also learnt from early mentors in other firms. As they put it:

He showed me that selling is really just a matter of problem-solving and putting yourself in the other person's shoes.

I felt that if I talked to him long enough I'd somehow find the secret of how he knew where to set up a new branch. It looked like magic, but I realized he always listened when other people talked about their business and where it was headed. ... This sort of talking isn't just chit-chat; it make you think about where you should be headed. I learnt eventually that it isn't magic, but a matter of constant alertness.

## The Value of Going Outside the Family Business

Regardless of which of the broad range of 'personal proficiency' skills were in question, our informants invariably said that the person who aspired to lead the firm first had to go outside the firm to acquire these skills. Why was this? After all, on the face of it, people who have grown up in a family business setting could learn these general personal and business skills within the context of their own firm. In fact, the experience would appear to be 'laid on'. Yet, as one of our informants put it when discussing the need to learn the personal discipline needed for business:

I would rather send them off to Sydney, to stay with another sister or somebody like that, and let them work for David Jones or Grace Brothers or somebody else for two years, to see what it's like working for somebody else in the retail trade. Where they can't just walk out the door and get in the car and go to the gym.

He, like our other informants, felt that getting outside experience was important for allowing future owners of family businesses to appreciate that the discipline needed to run a business was not just a requirement of their own family business. He expanded on this theme. In looking back on his own business training, the best thing he had gained by spending time away from the firm was:

Just seeing the way things work. Discipline is not quite the right word, but seeing the structure. That you have a boss that you are answerable to. You still have that thing when you come to a family business. You can't just be left with an open cheque book.

Davis and Tagiuri (1989) lend support to this viewpoint. Our informants consistently suggested that specific aspects of the experience needed to run family businesses had to be gained outside the business. Davis and Tagiuri (1989), in their study of father-son dyad relationships in family business, found strong evidence that sons should not start working with their fathers until father and son are both beyond their individual periods of identity formation. Not only must sons have time to establish their own identities away from their families, but the sons' presence might exacerbate the fathers' own questioning and internal conflicts. Thus certain periods and forms of learning need to be undertaken away from the family firm.

Leon and Katie Danco also endorse the need to learn self-discipline at an early stage and to develop it during the aspiring business leader's formal education. Certainly it is needed well before the aspiring family business leader enters the family business in any formal role.

> **Leon Danco**: I think the major thing these youngsters have to learn is self-discipline. With self-discipline, you can do anything you want. Without self-discipline, you will never be free. And if you have the self-discipline, if you have respect for the business, for how you are going to earn your living, and I think really that self-discipline is the most important thing. You start this when you are a child. But when you go away to the university, you got to have that self-discipline. If not, you are going to flunk out.

## *Where Outside?*

Owners of family owned businesses sometimes disagreed about *which* outside route should be followed to acquire business skills. For example, and in contrast to the Dancos' opinion, not everyone in our study was convinced that future family business owners needed to have studied business or some other course at University or a college of technical and further education. As we saw earlier, at least some owners are concerned that formal university studies are insufficient and even counterproductive for the context of the creative and practical sides of business. Nevertheless, many Australian family business owners have taken the route of tertiary study and they are doing so in increasing numbers. Smyrnios *et al.* (1999) in their *1999 Australian Family Business Lifestyle Audit*, found that slightly less than half of family business proprietors held tertiary qualifications: 46.9 per cent of small, 51.8 per cent of medium, and 55.8 per cent of large firm owners. About 30 per cent of proprietors held academic qualifications below matriculation (year 12). These findings are similar to the profile of family businesses internationally (Nager *et al.*, 1995).

Gaining a broad knowledge of the industry at a technical level is also best done early and outside the firm. In fact, several of the owners in our study said that they didn't have the time or the expertise to be training people. General business skills, that is, skills which are important in all businesses but which are not specifically related to the product or service of the particular business, should be acquired by prospective leaders before they arrive back in the family business. Examples of skills people need to learn outside were information technology skills, management skills, sales skills and product knowledge. One informant, the CEO of a major food production firm put it, recalled his own experience of learning the technical side of his business's products in this way:

> ... so at night, after work, I'd sometimes go and work in bakeries, just to learn how to handle dough, and what the terminology was. And then I went to Sydney and worked in the Bread Research Institute for a while and then set up a laboratory in Brisbane. We were about the first ones to come up with any form of quality control. I used to love it. I used to pack my swag and go up to Cairns. I'd make dough with the bakers, and try to persuade them to buy my flour. Then we introduced the idea of not merely having representatives going out to take flour orders, but also having technical representatives who were bakers. We trained them up to be salesmen, and they would not just take orders, but be there to advise.

Without knowing it at the time, this CEO was developing his entrepreneurial and sales skills as well as the technicalities of flour. Because the bakers he was talking to were in a 'downstream' business from the one his family firm was engaged in, he also gained a thorough appreciation of his customers' needs in addition to as issues such as quality control. While he was ostensibly learning 'technical/product' skills, learning them outside the family firm meant he could also master a variety of less obvious skills which in the long run would be important for running his own business.

## Problems With Learning Outside the Business

Just because family business owners agreed that going outside the firm was necessary didn't mean that the process was a simple one. There were a variety of potential problems arising from other people's perceptions of the learner. These perceptions could come from outside the firm or inside it – and sometimes both.

*Views From Outside the Firm – The Threat of Competition*

The CEO of the car sales business who had worked in another similar firm interstate said that while he had learned a great deal from his time there, he had always been aware of an undercurrent of suspicion of him as a potential future competitor:

> You couldn't call it rational. Most people don't go interstate to buy a car, so what they were showing me couldn't be used against them in a competition sense. But somehow, because they knew I would probably go back and work in the family firm eventually, they were a bit cautious in telling me the really good tricks of the trade.

*Views From Inside the Firm – More Competition*

Often, more problems arose when the learner returned to the firm. To begin with, it was frequently a problem to persuade others, especially older people in the firm, to believe in the learner's hard-won expertise. Jealousy in the family firm could arise if other members of the family felt the learner who had left the business would eventually return to a favoured position. This was also clear in the case of the car dealership business. As we mentioned, the owner had sent her son interstate the business to learn business from a top firm in the same industry. However, bringing him back into the firm was difficult. As the CEO said, summarizing the situation:

> This might sound odd, but everyone was very protective of their own job. They thought, if P. [*name of her son*] is going to take over the job of this, where am I going to be? If P. is going to take over the job of that, where's my job going to be? So he had to actually earn his way through. Not to take over anybody's job, but in not doing that he didn't have the responsibility, and wasn't able to learn that responsibility. He was working in a department rather than running a department. And this was very difficult. I know how the manager might feel, because they knew what he was to be groomed for, but they couldn't have him just sitting beside them all the time and they couldn't have him take over their job. […] So he was a bit like the ugly duckling. No-one wanted to pass on their skills, because they would put themselves in jeopardy.

As well as the jealousy issue, then, it seemed to our informants that many management jobs have a Catch-22 quality about them. That is, you can't learn management without doing it, but you can't be allowed to take management responsibilities without already having learnt. As the same female CEO explained about her son's difficulty in gaining experience inside the firm even after he had gained a great deal outside, the skills of running a department depend a great deal on the view others have of you:

**Interviewer**: So you felt you couldn't just put him into the position of running a department?

**Respondent**: He didn't have the skills to do it. You couldn't put an unskilled person in to run a department. You've got to have respect in your department. If you and your department are to work, you've got to have the respect of the people you are working with. I didn't say that he didn't have the skills, but he wasn't mature enough. It was a matter of maturity. So I couldn't take that risk.

The problem arises because management jobs such as running a department are very visible within the firm. The head of a department must have the respect of the people in the department, but this respect only comes from knowing how to do the job already. There is no easy solution to the problem; it seems only time can resolve it. In the present case, the CEO's son eventually ended up running the used car side of the business as an intermediate step. In this position he slowly gained both the respect of others in the business and the confidence of his mother:

It couldn't be done at any earlier age. Also, at that time I didn't have the confidence that he was showing the skills that I believed he needed. [...] That maturity certainly did come, but we went through a decade of very difficult times.

Leon Danco advises strongly against some of the conventional wisdom that suggests family members joining the firm should 'start at the bottom' to avoid accusations of nepotism:

**Leon Danco**: They [*the current owners of the business*] often think you [*the new family member joining the business*] need to start at the bottom like their old dad did, whether it is in the abattoir or as part of the construction crew or whatever your ground floor is. They have got to show that you don't have any privileges so you are going to work in the abattoir in the world's worst position. Just to show this you are going to work in a construction gang in the hottest day with the minimum tools. You are going to have jobs that are unbelievably miserable. Just because you are his kid, he can't let you think that you don't work from the bottom. But this is no use in a world where the leader's got to make major executive judgements at the age of forty. It means your basic qualification for leadership will be being a good meat cutter, or a good road machine handler, some minimum level work. What you do need is proper entry level skills for the business and the right attitudes formed. These things are best learned in a public company outside.

As a corollary to this, Leon Danco has some advice for those already in the family business about how to deal with the family member who has come back to work in the business at a level well above the bottom. It is to do the opposite of holding on to their own jobs and guarding their private knowledge:

> **Leon Danco**: And he [*the newcomer*] is coming into a reasonably middle level job – not at the bottom, not at the top. But he can call it a real job at that level and everybody expects a lot from him now. He is thirty years old. Assuming he finished his formal education at twenty-two, that typically gives him one hundred months of outside experience after the end of his normal academic activities. And he comes in and he has fifty year-old business executives running around, forty-five year-old business executives. They have been with dad for twenty years and along comes this kid. He is going to be their boss. 'You have two paths,' I tell these employees. 'You can sit there and point out every failure he makes if you want to make him look bad in front of the old man's eyes. But by doing this you gain the son's undying enmity so that when dad does move on by death, by resignation, or something, and once the son is in power, your job is not very secure. It'll be a case of "you have been beating me up for the last ten years, friend, so I am going to get even". And so it's in your best interest, whether you're the Vice-President of Sales, the Vice-President of Manufacturing, the Director of Purchasing, whoever you are in the second level of management – your best job security is to be this guy's best teacher'.

## *Looking Outside the Firm for Talent*

Our informants were convinced that it was vital for people learning the firm to go outside to learn business. The importance of this stage is reinforced by the face that many of them, especially younger CEOs, felt it was equally important that they consider outsiders as possible contenders for senior management positions in the family firm. In general, CEOs of family businesses in our study said they kept an eye on the developing skills of family members to see if they had potential to enter the upper management ranks. However they also all felt they should have the right to take on people from outside the firm if no-one inside it could do the job well enough.

The issue comes into sharper focus when some kind of expansion of the business is necessary. This is a common event in the adolescent stage of the business life cycle. For one of our informants, the CEO of a resort business, problems arose when he needed to decide between employing a family member and an outsider when plans were being made to open up a new line of business. The business had been extremely successful in the hospitality industry, but opening a major conference venue represented a major departure from the firm's traditional area of expertise. As this CEO said:

> I've said to them bluntly a number of times that no-one from the family can manage it because no-one has the skill. It's a pretty simple case. T. [*the informant's brother*] would be the closest, but T. couldn't do it. He's had experience in conferences, and food and beverage, but only limited experience. But he has no experience in marketing, and he's never opened a new business.

We will have more to say about this when we deal in detail with 'learning *our* business' in the next chapter. For now, however, let us simply note that learning outside is the primary focus of the first learning stage for the future owner, but that learning from the outside is a constant requirement of learning for the business.

## Going Even Further Outside

Some of the family business owners we spoke to said it was advisable for future members of the family owned business, including future owners, not merely to go away from the family business to learn their skills but to acquire them outside a family business situation. This could include learning in a different industry from the one of which the family business was a part. Accordingly, the view the learner would gain of the business context and its component variables would be extremely broad. This would give the learner a wider perspective and potentially improve the industry itself by injecting insights from different contexts. As our informant from the packaging industry put it:

> ... it's good when people from one industry go and look at what is happening in another industry, just to see if they are doing things which can be transferred to your own industry. You can become too focussed on your embedded environment. Hamill [*the author of* Competing for the Future, *the book our informant was reading at the time we interviewed him*] makes the point that we have to become experts in forgetting.

*Going Outside – Learning What Not To Do*

Finally, for some of our informants, going outside the family firm had been important simply to learn how *not* to do something. A third generation CEO of a firm in the hospitality industry related this aspect of his experience in this way:

> I think I was quite lucky working with [*name of the owner of another firm in the hospitality industry*] for a number of years. He was particularly successful in those years as a private businessman who ran his business in a pretty authoritarian manner. He ran it as centralized as they [*his father and his uncle, that is, the second generation members of his family owned business*] did. Maybe even more so, because there was only one of him. But he ran his business on much tougher business principles than they would, and he went to extremes. He taught me a lot on how not to handle staff. He had no time for training or multi-skilling. But on the business principles side he taught me a lot on how to run the business, how to look at efficiencies and costs and wages and that sort of thing, which they [*the respondent's father and uncle*] didn't really look at.

## Where is 'Outside the Firm' for Women?

We saw earlier that 'going outside the firm' sometimes involved even going outside the industry of the family business. This was often the case for women family business owners. For them, the settings in which they had learned their original, general skills were often far removed from their current business. One who now owns a motor dealership, had learned her people skills and her selling skills in cosmetics retailing. Another who runs a business in the hotel and conference management industry, reflected on the contribution of her nursing training to her current activities:

> You didn't make mistakes, and you were disciplined, and there were systems, and everybody kept to them. And it was just organised and well run. No mistakes. That's what I tell people here. You can't make mistakes.

So for women CEOs in our research sample, going outside takes on an additional twist. Most of our informants had started their career in an unrelated area, and had only held a support position 'inside' the business. This meant their skills were not recognized even by themselves until the opportunity – or rather the necessity – to run the business arose. As one of our informants put it:

I was always involved a little, particularly in the early stages when he [*her late husband, and the former CEO of the business*] was still in the Police. I used to answer the phone. And I always helped as much as I could. I enjoyed it all. And I can remember working when I had that number four baby. In those days it wasn't seen to be the right thing to be working when you were pregnant, and I can remember both of us being embarrassed by the fact that I was helping in the business and pregnant at the same time. I became fully involved really, only when I was widowed.

Another female CEO, discussing her late husband's attitude to her role in the family business, said:

He saw me as a support, but never saw me running it. I would never have expected to, either. I never had it in my mind that I would be anything but a support.

So women had often been part of the business for a long time, and also had acquired many of the necessary skills outside it. Despite this however, they were not thought of as the logical choice for the top job in the same way as men who had gone outside the firm and then returned to it. In short, there is a lack of a clear strategic progression in women CEOs' careers of the kind many authors describe as typical and desirable in family business (see, for example Barach *et al.* 1988; Bork, 1986; Danco, 1982; Harvey and Evans, 1994; Jaffe, 1990; Ward, 1987). Most of our female informants would have had no experience of Leon Danco's recommendation that moving into the firm be a planned event. For the women in our study, getting to the top has been the result of 'just being there' when the occasion demanded rather than moving inexorably up the ladder. In their own view and that of other people, women business owners in family business had *found themselves* taking over the business by default rather than consciously or unconsciously directing themselves towards it as seems characteristic of male CEOs in our sample.

Because of others' perception that they had always 'just been there' without really having an impact on the business, women CEOs sometimes later had had to act in a more entrepreneurial way than was typical for the second generation in a family owned business. This is clear from several women CEOs' accounts of how they had quietly pushed the business forward, creating new business though usually from a 'behind the scenes' position:

We started with a staff of thirty-five people, who came from all parts of Queensland. We had to start a service division, a parts division, sales, etc. In those times I came in and worked on the switch, and worked as the general roustabout. I used to do the car registration. I used to get in the car and try to get the tyre dealerships and little garages all the way up the north coast to buy their spare parts from [*name of the interviewee's firm*]. That freed up B. [*the respondent's husband*] to run things here. I worked in spare parts, and I used to work in service, doing the filing, etc. I did everything I could do to help. I wasn't in every day, but most days I was in. I still had a young family then.

This phenomenon of women's less strategic progress may be an artefact of the particular age cohort of these interviewees and their firms, however. The 1999 *Australian Family Business Lifestyle Audit* (Smyrnios *et al.*, 1999) reported that slightly over seven per cent of family business owners were women. That represented an increase of almost one and a half times the results of the equivalent 1997 survey.

Despite this apparent difference between male and female CEOs' ways of entering the firm, both genders now held broadly similar views about the ways family businesses should be learnt and run. If anything women CEOs are even more firmly convinced than men about the kinds of skills needed to run '*our* business', that is the *family* business, and how these should be learnt. We will say more about this in the next chapter.

## The Paradox for Family Firms: The Inside versus the Outside

This 'inside-outside' dimension to getting the basics of business knowledge is at the heart of the first paradox about learning family business: what we will call the 'inside-outside' paradox. We might think of it as something like the Biblical parable of the prodigal son, who leaves his father's house and eventually returns, but only after disappearing for a long time, wasting his inheritance and being virtually given up for lost. In a similar way, 'going outside' in order eventually to 'return inside' the firm later is both a vital opportunity for learning and a potential threat to the family nature of the business. It is vital to learning since the younger generation needs to develop skills and gain perspectives they cannot acquire by staying in the family business. They also need to prove themselves worthy of a place in the senior management structure of the firm. But it is also a threat to the survival of the firm *as a family firm*, because the person who leaves the family business setting to learn about how to run a business may in the end never come home.

Virtually all our informants had at some earlier time contemplated the possibility – even the probability – that they might not ever work in the family firm. Most often this was in the early stages of learning business. The CEO of an award-winning packaging firm, when asked whether he had always envisaged being in the company, said:

> No. The year I graduated from high school, 1965, half the company was sold off to [*name of a major firm in a related industry*]. At that stage I was just starting my apprenticeship, and I said to my father, 'Well, there goes my opportunity for the future. You've just gone and sold half the company'.

> So I went off and did my own thing. I wasn't aggro about it. I just said that I would do my own thing. And I did my own training and education, and worked for other companies in all sorts of senior positions, then went out as a consultant. What I'm leading up to is that the reason I've taken this company on is because I've done my own thing. It hasn't been structured towards this, but it's now emerging that I have the necessary tools to take the company on. I've had a lot of leadership exposure. I've been the president of half a dozen different organizations, and been leading change in those organizations. And I've been leading change as a consultant.

This view of the situation makes the inside-outside paradox particularly clear. This CEO is now able to lead the company precisely because he originally envisaged *not* doing so and sought to develop his business skills and build a career elsewhere. He achieved this in ways that made him demonstrably competent as a business leader in other situations, and therefore qualified him as competent to lead the family firm. His approach was typical of the views expressed by our informants. The CEO in this example went on to explain that it had been difficult for him to enter the family firm. Although he had been a member of the family firm's board while working elsewhere, he had seen himself as merely an external director. Moreover, he had found himself outvoted on every attempt to get change for the better. Even now, this CEO only expects to stay with the family firm for a few years, only long enough to turn it around after a period of difficulty. This is unusual however; he was the only CEO in our sample to envisage leaving the family firm once he had returned to it.

## Pathways Through the 'Inside-Outside' Paradox

Despite the difficulties, there seemed to be only one viable pathway through the inside-outside paradox: 'go outside anyway'. It seemed to be generally accepted that future managers of family owned businesses had to leave that business at an early stage so that they would be equipped to come back into the firm later. The business owners in our sample recommended this course of action universally, regardless of the stage of the organizational life cycle the firm had reached. It simply never disputed that family business owners needed to have gained experience outside at least for an extended period. Nevertheless, as we will see shortly, the stage of the family firm in terms of the business life cycle affects the relevance of the location where the outside experience is gained. If the family firm is moving towards maturity then experience and learning outside the firm that assists the family firm to make that transition is highly beneficial.

Dealing with the necessity to leave the family firm has a number of consequences for members of the family business, such as the need to accept uncertainty and keeping the route back to the family firm open.

### *Accepting Uncertainty*

As we said in the first chapter, the paradoxes that arise about learning the family business can only be managed or dealt with, not eliminated. In line with this, there was a general agreement that inside-outside paradox could not be avoided. The pathway through the paradox was 'just do it'. The consequences of this are only vaguely defined. One approach is for both the younger and the older generations in the family business simply to accept the uncertainty of not knowing whether a member of the younger generation will eventually return to take over the business. This is difficult for many CEOs of family businesses. As we saw in the first chapter, the interest in handing on the business to a member of the family is, for many people, what defines the business as a family one. So the appeal of creating something that will carry on after them and be maintained within their family is very strong for most CEOs:

> Like every father, I'd like to hand something on to my son. I'd like to hand on something that has been handed on to me – an ongoing, viable business that's proud of the name it carries.

Another CEO, looking back on the continuity issue from the perspective of the younger generation, puts it this way:

> When I first came here, I started in Dispatch. I was never going to join this family business. I was going to do something else. I was at University attending lectures for sixteen hours a week, working as a waiter at the Greek Club thirty-six hours a week, and playing golf five days a week. It was great for my handicap. In fact I went from twenty-two to six in about twelve months. But what I was doing was wrong. I was wasting time. I had a long talk to my Dad. He told me about how he'd like to see the succession happen and I joined him and haven't regretted it. It's been great.

## Keeping the Route Back to the Family Firm Open

In the cases we are discussing, members of both the older and the younger generations had at some point accepted the possibility that the firm might not continue as a family firm. In fact in one case, this had seemed almost inevitable when half the firm was sold to another company. Moreover, as the CEO of that firm said, it is important not to be upset or 'aggro' about it. For him, dealing with the need for potential leaders of the family business to go outside the firm the pathway consists of quietly keeping all options open for the next generation to return and take over the business. His father had not done this with him, and in some ways had resisted his return. Now, with his own son, he is having to deal with the same issue. In an early instance of how CEOs may strategically select forms of learning outside the firm, this CEO is determined to make sure the matter is worked out differently. He is starting early on planning options to make sure his son – a potential third generation owner – eventually has the opportunity and the ability to work in the family firm.

**Respondent**: My son is into high school now and he's always had a bit of trouble with maths. It's a confidence thing, mainly. ...

**Interviewer**: That would be a pretty important skill in this kind of business, wouldn't it?

**Respondent**: Yes. You couldn't do without it. He'd need other training too, of course, probably engineering. But there's no way you can get to do engineering without a good score in maths. So, not that I'm telling him he's got to join the firm, I've organized him some private tutoring in maths. A good thing too – he was on the point of giving it up completely – doing none at all in the last two years [*of school*]. He's doing a lot better now. Of course I'm not doing this just to make sure he goes into the firm, but at least it means he's not prevented from coming in by not having this basic knowledge. …

It might be thought that being a son or daughter of the CEO is one pathway through the 'inside-outside' paradox – a kind of insurance that someone from the younger generation will enter the firm eventually. But in fact this is far from true. A number of our informants had at some stage been uncertain whether they would return to the business. Moreover, virtually all our informants noted how they had needed to 'prove themselves first'. They were equally firm that they would require the same of the next generation. So it is clear that there are several reasons that the family firm might not continue as a family firm. First, simply being a member of the next generation is no guaranteed pathway to eventually running the family business, rather the opposite. Second, the younger generation may regard the family firm as only one of many career prospects. Acquiring specific business skills may mean choosing a permanent career that is not related to the family business. Finally, present CEOs believe they should be permitted to recruit specific skills from outside the family if they wish. The combination of the two factors threatens the continuity of the business as a family business.

**Summary and Conclusion**

From our research, the first 'personal proficiency' priority in learning family business is to learn personal management, particularly the self-discipline that leadership will eventually require. People skills were also vital. Unexpectedly, the technical skills of business were of lesser importance, but nonetheless were not to be overlooked and our informants insisted on a range of general business skills that they thought future leaders of the family business needed to learn.

The common theme to learning these skills and attitudes was that they had to be acquired outside the business. In fact, and Leon and Katie Danco stressed this, some of the most fundamental of the necessary attitudes and skills were learned so early in life that the future business owner could not have really been aware that he or she was absorbing attitudes and viewpoints that would later equip them for business leadership. These attitudes included self-reliance and a positive approach to being in business for oneself.

The first paradox of learning the family business setting appeared as learners tried to fulfil the personal management and business proficiency priorities. That is, learners in this first stage invariably needed to go *outside* the business. This was not because the skills needed for good personal management or for general business proficiency were not apparent within the family firm. Learners at this stage needed to go outside because of the need to be seen as credible as a business person both by people within the family firm and by others, whether competitors or people in firms linked to the family business in some other way. Most importantly, perhaps, future family business owners needed to be credible in their own eyes.

The learning may sometimes have seemed negative, such as learning what not to do from watching the incompetent performance of managers outside the family firm. It sometimes had special problems. For example it was sometimes difficult to learn skills that other firms knew would present a competitive threat in the future, and to convince other people in the family firm that the learner had really learned enough to take a management role in the family firm. There were occasional variations to the 'going outside' rule. One was 'going even further outside' – that is, as far as other industries. This suggested an even greater possibility that the learner will choose a career that will take him or her permanently away from the family business. Another was the kind of 'going outside' that women business owners frequently experienced. That is, women owners of family business – and male members of the business also – often saw themselves as 'having always been outside'. Often, they had little idea of the considerable skills they had acquired through observation and the backroom support they had provided over many years.

These issues may also arise in non-family firms. However from the family firm's perspective, the 'go outside' rule has a special paradox – the person who leaves to learn the skills needed for leading a business may be tempted to choose never to return to the family firm. For true learning to occur, the eventual leader of the family firm has to have been something of a 'prodigal son'. Just as the father of the Biblical prodigal son seemed to have lost his son forever, there are no guarantees that the 'prodigal son' who leaves the family business setting will necessarily come back.

The pathway through this paradox: 'go outside anyway', even at the risk of losing the family nature of the firm, seems to be a general one. That is, it is a pathway independent of the stage in the business life cycle that the firm has reached. Perhaps it is because the general skills that are vital for business, personal management skills, people skills and a variety of technical skills, are just that – general skills. Learning in general is learning that does not change depending on the stage of development of a particular firm. Nevertheless, the forms and locations of learning chosen, if the choices are made strategically, could be influenced by the stage the family has reached, or which the incumbent CEO wishes it to achieve.

The next stage of learning tells a different story from that of acquiring general business skills. Just as the learners have acquired a knowledge of themselves, of other people, and of business in general, it becomes important for them to adapt and modify this knowledge to take account of the special demands and qualities of family business, and *their* family business in particular. In this learning stage, the business life cycle moves out of the background and starts to shape the learning. How this happens is the subject of our next chapter: 'Learning *Our* Business'.

## References

Barach, J. A., Gantisky, J., Carson, J. A. and Doochin, B. A. (1988), 'Entry of the next generation: Strategic challenges for family business', *Journal of Small Business Management*, vol. 21, no. 1, pp. 49-56.

Bork, David (1986), *Family Business, Risky Business: How to Make It Work*, New York, American Management Association.

Danco, L. (1982), *Beyond Survival: A Business Owner's Guide for Success*, Cleveland, Ohio University Press.

Davis, John A. and Tagiuri, R. (1989), 'The Influence of Life Stage on Father-Son Work Relationships in Family Companies', *Family Business Review*, vol. 2, no. 1, Spring, pp. 47-74.

Harvey, M. and Evans, R. E. (1994), 'The Impact of Timing and Mode of Entry on Successor Development and Successful Succession', *Journal of Family Business*, vol. 7, no. 3, Fall, pp. 221-37.

Jaffe, D. (1990), *Working with the ones you love*, Berkeley, CA, Conari Press.

Nager, K., Aronoff, Craig E. and Ward, John L. (1995), *American Family Business Survey: 1995*, Arthur Andersen Center for Family Business, 711 Louisiana, Suite 1300, Houston, TX.

Smyrnios, K., Romano, R. and Pashias, G. (1999), *The 1999 Family Business Lifestyle Audit*, Melbourne, Monash University and Family Business Australia.

Ward, John L. (1987), *Keeping the Family Business Healthy: How to Plan for Continuing Growth, Profitability, and Family Leadership*, San Francisco, Jossey-Bass.

# Chapter 4

# Learning *Our* Business

In the previous chapter, we saw that family business owners agreed how it important it was to learn general self-management, people skills and other general business skills during the first phase of learning the family business. They also pointed out – virtually always – the need for the person learning the business to leave the family business to do this. This gave rise to a paradox peculiar to family businesses, a paradox we called the 'inside-outside' paradox. In brief, the 'inside-outside' paradox pointed out that going outside the firm to learn how best to run it was necessary, even vital for the firm's survival. However doing so was also a threat – it meant that the continuity of the firm as a family firm came under threat.

It turns out that learning these general skills is not enough, however. In fact there were frequent suggestions from our informants that something more than a general business grounding is needed to run a family owned business. That is, there is something about learning *our* business that is different from learning business in general. What is it about *our* business that seemed to be of special value? And there is a new paradox. It arises from the question of how you maintain a sense of sameness, of continuity that allows owners and customers alike to see the business as 'the same' family business – at the same time as it is dealing with a rapidly changing world. This chapter is about what makes learning *our* business special.

## Family Business is Postgraduate Study

In the previous chapter Leon and Katie Danco pointed out how much learning about the value of *our* business – the family business – takes place before people are consciously aware of it. Future leaders need to acquire a set of attitudes and values from their parents and a range of other people. They also need to gain experience of formal learning and other businesses to equip them to run the family business. But what about when the first stage of learning general skills is completed? At some point the learner has completed the stage of learning which gives them self-discipline, people skills, technical skills for business, all of which – at least in time – will give them the capacity to gain others' respect. At that stage, typically, the learner finds himself or herself returning to the family business.

According to Davis and Tagiuri (1989), this stage needs to be handled carefully, and it should be undertaken only at a time which respects the identity formation needs of both the older generation (typically the father) and the younger (typically the son). Yet it cannot be neglected. According to many of our informants, at some point it seemed that the armoury of skills, attitudes, abilities and personal qualities acquired outside the firm is still in need of refinement. Something else, something at a further level, now needs to be learned. As Leon Danco puts it: 'Family business is postgraduate study' and the structure of family businesses in the United States is starting to reflect this in a formal way. As Leon Danco points out, many family businesses in the United States have councils which impose steep entry requirements on members of the family who are seeking to return to and learn the family business:

> **Leon Danco**: The successors [*to the family business*] learn by watching at a higher level in the second and the third generations. [...] They [*the councils of many family businesses*] have a requirement for five years of minimum outside experience and a managerial position gained in the outside after two jobs. There's a whole bunch of requirements. You have to have this, this, and this before you take the postgraduate course called 'The Family Business'. The family business is the world's worst place to teach elementary anything.

Many family business owners echo these sentiments, but more than skills, and ability to cut it in the outside world, they stress something else: tradition. Steven Schmidheiny, a leading Swiss owner manager of a fourth generation family enterprise with a strong international background, says that ownership of a business entails a sense of responsibility. It is a privilege, even a 'noble duty, a responsibility to carry out, to perform'. Put simply, the family business tends to perpetuate values.

> **Schmidheiny**: It is obvious that family enterprises have a more important element of tradition than most corporations. It is extremely important, on the one hand, to respect traditions because they are an integral element of family companies.

So what are these postgraduate lessons in the family business? And how are they to be learned? For our informants, they seemed to be about the values of the family business and ensuring they continued into the future.

## Learning Priority: Perpetuating Values

Our research suggests that what the younger generation learnt from the older generation, even before joining the firm, was mostly at the level of broad principle. For example, many CEOs pointed out their fathers' capacity for hard work and determination. In another typical example a CEO acknowledged his father's capacity to admit when he had made a mistake. He describes his father and how he learned from him in this way:

> I didn't actually listen and make notes. I found him extremely straight. If he made a mistake he would say, 'That was wrong, I got the wrong flour'. And he'd replace it. He wouldn't beat around the bush and blame somebody else. It's those simple things that you learn, the same way as children learn.

He has adopted this practice himself and also uses his father's low-key approach to imparting these skills to others:

> If I go down to see the general manager of Coles or Woolworths, Franklins or any of the majors, I'll usually take someone with me so that they can see. And they can learn by my mistakes too! And after it's over we don't have a formal debriefing, but we have a discussion over a beer or over dinner that night. I don't think it would help, for example, to send out a screed every week to tell people how to behave or how to do things.

According to Leon Danco, the same approach applies at the next stage of learning, that is, when the member of the younger generation enters the family business and begins to work there. A lot of knowledge has already come from the younger generation learning from the older by general observation and unconscious absorption, and this form of learning continues once the younger family member enters the firm. However, once this stage has been reached, Danco argues the members of the older generation – including the founder – have to be prepared to actively share the issues with the more junior member:

> **Leon Danco**: The child comes with these good and bad skills, with all sorts of good and bad baggage. In the best of all possible worlds, the father has stayed close to his son.[1] He has shared information with his son as someone he is trying to explain the future to. He is trying to explain what he – the son – should be thinking about, and sharing his problems with his children. The communication between father, leader, and son, follower, should have started a long time ago.

[...]

What he ought to do is to start sharing with his son some of the joys of the business as the son becomes an increasingly articulate listener. The son now knows what cashflow means. The son now knows what inventory liquidation is. If he is really learning from his boss where he is, his father now becomes a lecturer in the problems of his own company, the good, the bad, the losses, and the great joy when we win something. And so then the son comes into the business, there won't be any questions like, 'Now, which way is the men's room? How many people do we have working for us?'. After all, the son is not a stranger. He has been more than a bystander during the three, four, five or even ten years he has been away.

Often, sharing knowledge, emotions and values can be difficult, especially if the issue of the older generation's retirement has not been resolved or if the father feels under pressure to retire. As Leon Danco says:

**Leon Danco**: A twenty-two year-old man can get to thirty-two and Dad will still be only sixty. He still isn't ready to be moved over. Unfortunately, children seem to feel that once they get into the family business, the next step is Dad's retirement. That's not necessarily something for discussion right away. Dad is not going to retire. A thirty year-old son has a fifty-five year-old, sixty year-old father. Dad has spent his whole life building this up and the son has to solve Dad's problems first. And in the same way the son should be coming into a job that has almost been created in anticipation of his arrival. It's a planned move. The guy doesn't just show up at the factory door and say, 'Father, I'm here. Where is my office?'. He should be coming into a job that is needed, has been thought about, and has been discussed.

### The Use of Debt – a Vehicle for Values

In the first stage of learning we have already seen something of the values that get passed down between one generation and the next. First, and perhaps most importantly, there is simply the pleasure of achievement that comes from being in business and from seeing the gains that are to be made from hard work, from taking responsibility for oneself and for continuing to learn in the business. Then there is the notion that the business, especially because it is a family business, is something special, something worthy of being passed down from one generation to another. But how are the values of the business and of the people in it to be perpetuated as life cycle stages – and hence the needs of the business – change? How family firms handle debt turned up frequently in our research as an example of this problem and the ways family businesses handle it. To begin with, let us examine what other research shows about family owned businesses' use of debt.

## The 'Strategic Conservatism' of Family Business

The prevailing conventional wisdom of academic researchers and family business consultants alike is that family businesses are typically not interested in sharing ownership with shareholders outside the family. Their financial policies typically lead them to minimize the risk of losing independence. This is seen in their preference for retained earnings or bank loans over outside equity finance to finance growth. This has been described as family firms' 'strategic conservatism' (Dunn, 1995). Researchers frequently point out that this is a viable funding strategy in relatively stable competitive environments, but is less sustainable in highly competitive and volatile markets where growth needs are more urgent.

The 'strategic conservative' approach means that family firms face challenges at both strategic and attitudinal levels. Family firm responses range from pursuing non-growth strategies with a reduced demand for funding, to continuing growth but linking this with a willingness to revise the family business management's view on how acceptable non-family equity might be.

There is empirical evidence for family firms' adherence to 'strategic conservativism'. McConaughy and Phillips (1999), in a recent study of family firms which included both founder-controlled and descendant-controlled businesses, found that family firms used less debt than do non-family businesses. This is consistent with the difference between family and non-family firms that the 'strategic conservative' approach would predict. More than this, however, McConaughy and Phillips found that when the age of founder-controlled and descendant-controlled firms was held constant, founder-controlled businesses did not differ significantly from descendant-controlled family firms in their leverage policies. Thus the attitude to the use of debt does seem to be a value which is passed on from the older to the younger generation.

Poutziouris (2001) had similar results from a survey in the UK of 240 small and medium sized firms' use of venture capital. He found that family firms in the sample financed their operations following the 'pecking order' theory. That is, they preferred first to use internally available funds, followed by debt, followed by venture capital. They were especially reluctant to use venture capital for research and development, or growth, or to make the firm more appealing to potential investors. Reasons for owner managing directors' reluctance to use venture capital centred around their concern about displacing family managers with outsiders, and their feeling that they lacked knowledge about the mechanics and rules of the venture capital deals (Poutziouris, 2001, p. 287).

Despite the traditional adherence of family firms to independence and the associated slower growth, recent evidence suggests that family firms may be adapting their strategies and changing their attitudes. For example, research in Australia published by *Yellow Pages* (1995) showed that only eight per cent of family owned businesses plan to grow significantly and 31 per cent do not wish to grow at all. However, this still indicates that close to 70 per cent of family owned businesses intended to grow either moderately or more significantly. Research by Dunn and Hughes (1995) into Scottish and Northern Irish family firms showed that many have changed their attitudes on the acceptability of non-family equity funding. The work by Moores and Mula (1996) on strategic conservatism in Australian family firms, also showed that many more families are in fact prepared to accept 'outside' shareholders to fund growth of their firms than the conventional wisdom might predict.

Given these changes in family firms' approach to debt over time, it is not surprising that in our study we found the younger generation of family business owners took a different view of debt compared to that of the older generation. In fact, our respondents' views on the use of debt illustrated clearly how the younger generation tends to make quite some changes to the older generation's management strategy when they begin to have some influence. Yet they did not see these changes as a real departure from what they had learned in terms of family business values. Let us see what the use of debt in our study had to say about learning *our* business.

*Debt – A Way of Teaching Values*

The majority of the firms in our sample had made cautious use of bank debt or other external sources of funds in the early start-up phases or to finance subsequent growth. In some instances the present CEO, looking back over events which were sometimes many years in the past, was vague about the extent to which debt had been used in earlier times and for what purpose. But nonetheless, the older generation's general approach to debt had been observed by the younger generation, and adopted at least at some level. As one younger generation CEO put it:

**Respondent**: We've always worked on bank overdrafts, of course. But my father has never. ... We probably could have owned far more properties, I suppose, or assets. But he would never borrow any more than he knew he could cover if anything went wrong. That's always been his policy, and he's taught us that. You never borrow any more than you can handle. If things go bad, and interest rates go up higher, your repayments are huge. Well, we've seen so many people come in, make a huge splash and go out as well, owing big money to people.

**Interviewer**: So it's conservative borrowing?

**Respondent**: Conservative, and we've been National Bank customers for fifty-six years.

This view was typical of most of our respondents. Even in later generations debt was often used reluctantly, even when the present CEO knew it was needed to achieve growth. In some instances, the approach to debt used by the younger generation was associated with bitter memories of the heavy-handed approach by the lending institutions of the time. One CEO recalled a period in his early life when his father had secured a loan to help the fledgling firm through a period of difficulty:

Every day they [*a representative of the bank*] used to come down and pick up the petty cash from the office to help pay off the debt. Eventually it was paid off, and my father always had a policy from then that no bank manager was going to set foot in the door. He would never go into debt. That was a good thing. It gave us a good financial base, but it meant that we didn't grow very much in that period of time.

With another firm, as soon as possible after the growth phase, the company was restructured so as to retire the debt. Even though debt was now used, and in amounts which the present CEO felt would have surprised and even alarmed his father, the founder, it was only allocated to areas which would generate immediate income.

*Debt – A Way of Imposing Values*

While debt was generally used conservatively, it had sometimes been a source of contention even between members of the older generation. While there might be broad philosophies about how to use it, there can still be tussles and minor struggles for power. This emerged in the case of a female CEO who had had only a minor role in the management of the firm when it started out. She, rather than her husband, had amassed the necessary equity, or rather the appearance of equity, in order to start the firm. This took quite some creativity and, as her account of it shows.

> We had so little equity that it was very hard to start. [...] We had to have $20,000 personally, that was F's [*name of the wider organization*] requirement. That was not including borrowings. So we sold our little house in Alderley, in which we had very little equity anyway, and the man that bought it gave us $2,000, a utility and a caravan. We put the caravan on the lot here, and traded in the utility. We borrowed a bit of money from our families, which was difficult to do! And we managed to arrange the balance sheet to make it look as if we had $20,000, but we didn't really.

The discussion here suggests the decision was taken jointly with her husband. However, it soon emerged that our informant was the prime mover in the decision and that it was taken partly against her husband's better judgement.

> He was certainly nervous about it – more than I was, probably. He always said to me that he didn't want us to bite off more than we could chew, but I could tell even then that it was now or never. If we hadn't taken the plunge then, maybe we never would have. And then we'd have always wondered whether we'd lost the opportunity to go it on our own.

At that stage, using debt was a way of presenting an appearance of solidity to the outside organization which controlled entry into the business. But ever since then, this same informant has recommended caution in the use of others' funds.

> I've never wanted my sons to think this is something they can do lightly. They are beholden to people and I don't want anyone to think we don't respect others' hard work as much as our own. We've seen plenty in this business who've come in, set up and disappeared, owing people big money. That's not for us, and it won't be for them [*her children*] either.

In some cases withholding access to debt becomes a justification for not rewarding the younger generation too early or too generously. In that way it becomes a way for the older generation to maintain control over the future of the business, particularly if there are several members of the younger generation. As one CEO put it:

I can recall people saying to my father – one old friend of ours who was a judge, for example – how are you ever going to keep the boys from fighting? He said that the best way was to keep them all very busy and pretty poor!

So even though the older generation could recall having had a hard time securing money for expansion or to ensure their founding role in the business, they don't necessarily allow the next generation access to funds from within the business or elsewhere so that they can do something similar. If anything, the opposite is true. This sometimes has to do with the need to control potential conflict arising from competing claims among members of the younger generation, as we saw in the previous example. The same female CEO who had had to create the appearance of having sufficient equity to buy into an independent business, had subsequently insisted on a strictly commercial basis for selling part of the business to one of her sons. She required a sale at full market rates even though he was the only one of her children to show real interest and aptitude in the business:

It's taken me twelve months to bed down the deal with P. [*the interviewee's son*]. He was looking at trying to get a bargain, and I was looking at a commercial transaction. [...] There has been a bit of to and fro, and anger, but it's a matter of learning to keep your cool with the family. With the other two there were certain jealousies and envies because P.'s got it now.

In still other cases, the younger generation has managed to persuade the older generation to take on some additional debt. This was always a difficult task. Once achieved, however, the member of the younger generation used debt to negotiate their right to run the firm, or some significant part of it. Sometimes this enabled the younger generation to force an expansion or a new strategic direction for the business. This in turn was part of demonstrating the younger generation's capacity to run the business. Recalling this situation, one (younger generation) CEO said:

I remember that when he finally lent me the money, he hadn't really wanted to do it. He did it only because I argued long and hard; he would probably say I wouldn't give him any peace until he agreed. In the end he said, 'I'll only take on the debt if you'll manage the new Brisbane venture'. He thought that this would be an end to the matter. Instead, it spurred me on. I knew the business needed to move interstate, and it gave me the chance to prove this and that I was the person to do it.

## The Paradox of Perpetuating Values: 'Continuing Differently'

These examples of the use of debt in family firms show the paradox that comes with learning *our* business. Learning *our* business means getting beyond the general skills that were learned in the first stage and appreciating what is special about *this* business. As a family business, this means 'perpetuating values'. In short, a particular set of values – both business values and personal values – are there to be learned, cherished and passed on. But because of the growth needs of the firm change as its position on the life cycle curve alters, the values are likely to be 'continued differently'. That is, the values of the family business – including a basically conservative approach to debt – are absorbed so that the learner feels that they are part of something special about *our* business. Because the values are special, because they add something, they should be continued. But this is not to say that everything is done in just the same way as the older generation would have done it. Stephen Schmidheiny, quoted at the outset of this chapter, went on to point out about family business values and traditions, that:

> … you must feel free to interpret them in the light of new developments. […] Although I did many things against my father's declared statements of principle, I know he would have done the same thing in my place; he has told me so. *Accepting* tradition is an important element, but feeling the freedom to interpret traditions in the light of the world as it is today and not as it was when tradition was formed is very important.

## Pathways Through the Paradox of 'Continuing Differently'

So in learning *our* business and its values, our participants yet again found themselves saying the business was 'the same, only different' from other businesses. There were two main pathways by which our informants 'valued values – but differently' as they came to grips with learning 'our' business. The first was to maintain the broad management philosophy of the previous generation rather than the detail of their strategies. The second was to recognize and develop the special market value of a family business.

### Pathway 1: Keep Strategic Philosophies Not Details

As we saw, the second and later generations in the family business have learned to value the principles of *our* business. This includes a number of broad principles for running a business, such as a cautious, even tight-fisted approach to debt, and personal qualities such as the capacity for self-discipline, honesty and hard work. The younger generation sticks with these ideas even though they pursue different firm strategies from the ones the older generation would have adopted. The values – and their new interpretation of them – is shown by the respect the younger generation has for the older generation's caution with debt, and yet their insistence that a certain level of debt is necessary for growth. As we saw, many if not most of our informants also admired the personal qualities of the older generation CEO. They had learned from him or her how to appreciate the values of hard work, discipline, honesty and endurance – and a proper caution with debt. Perhaps these things are best learnt from the experience of working inside the family business. Sometimes the broad values of the family firm were the most durable aspects of learning when the detail of running a firm needs to change rapidly.

*Pathway 2: Learn the Market Value of Family Business Values*

There is another pathway through the paradox of 'continuing differently' where the idea of 'valuing values' gains a new meaning. It has to do with discovering the *market* value of family business values. The CEO who drove a hard bargain but finally settled the family business on her son illustrates this second pathway. She said selling the business to a family member allowed her to stay involved, which selling it to someone else would not have allowed. So the business remains visibly a family business and she remains an active part of it. This has value not only in her eyes but, more especially, in the eyes of customers:

> It would have been much easier to sell it to Joe Bloggs, but to sell it to Joe Bloggs would have pushed me right out of it, which I didn't really want. I still want to be able to be here. As P. said himself, I would work with the staff better than he would. They are enjoying still seeing me here – the visibility of somebody they've seen around for a long time. It makes a link to the family thing. It makes it more family orientated than if I simply disappeared off the face of the earth. This way I can keep my office.

Owners of family businesses in our sample didn't need a transition between owners of the business to be aware of the '(market) value of values'. As the owner of a fruit and vegetable business said about his customers' perceptions of his business:

I think that with us, there's a feeling that if I'm not here there's one of my sons or one of my nephews, and I think we've been able to establish a good reputation for quality, for a determination to be as good as if not better than our competitors, in spite of not having the finance to do some of the things they can do. I think our integrity is pretty well intact.

Being seen to be a family business was important even when it was more a matter of perception than of reality. The realities could alter, such as when firms began to make increasing use of professional management, and the proportion of non-family to family members changed. This was clear from the situation of one of the businesses in our sample, which had recently had a major influx of professional staff. The business is a mountain resort, now in its fourth generation of owners. The founders, two brothers who were both more than ninety years old at the time of our research, were still to be seen on the premises. Now, however, they spent most of their time enjoying the sun on the verandah or making toast for the guests. But they were visible and active in the business, particularly in the eyes of customers. The current CEO, a grandson of the original founders, put it this way:

People still come up here and still feel that it's a family business. In fact guests have much more chance of meeting the family now. V. and P. [*the two founders*] turn up in the morning and cook the toast, and people say, 'Isn't it great?'. And they go to the bar just before dinner and have a drink with the guests, and the guests say, 'Isn't it great to see the family business still going here?'. But the reason they can do that is that they [*the older generation*] aren't doing the hard work that they used to do.

With firms developing export markets or joint ventures with overseas firms, the valuing the family aspect of the business has been an important part of their strategy. For one firm in our sample, exporting into China was made easier by the Chinese people's traditional respect for families and familiarity with family business. For another, selecting a joint venture partner was simplified by the fact that each recognized and admired in the other a speed of decision-making that was partly due to both of them being family businesses:

We didn't have a long relationship before we got together. We met the two brothers, and spent time with the people there, talked to people who were associated with them. But we made a fairly quick decision. We knew what we *didn't* want, and we found that their way of doing business was similar to ours.

These similarities in organizational culture that they both recognized as being part of a family business included:

> A very easy line of making decisions. Not a lot of political posturing to worry about. We talked, considered, decided and did. They have three thousand people, but they can make a decision as easily as we can.

These views are broadly consistent with some agency theorists' views that reduction in agency costs leads to family firms outperforming non-family firms (see, for example, McConaughy, 1994). Despite this, the CEO of this firm was not convinced that being run by a family makes any necessary difference to how well a firm is managed:

> I think there are people who are very professional and do a very good job even though they are not family. There are many very good managers, managing directors etc that provide all of that and are not family. So it gets down to the individual. To a degree, if the family business has performed well, they get some sense of security with the ownership of the business. However a well-managed, well-driven, private or public company with a good management structure can achieve the same result. I don't put too much down to the family aspect.

## The Dark Side of 'Valuing Values': Moving Insiders Out of the Family Firm

So far, this chapter has showed that learning *our* business has a lot to do with learning to recognize, value and perpetuate the values associated with being a family business. This is despite the fact that these values often need to be perpetuated *differently*. But there is sometimes a more difficult issue to be considered. Many of our informants at some point had had to consider the issue of who is to be part of 'our' business. Perhaps because of the recognized value of being a family firm, in both the personal and the market sense of the term, many of the more difficult experiences connected with learning *our* business were associated with determining whether certain members of the family should remain in it. This dilemma had often marked their accession to the top position, but not always. One CEO recalled a struggle between himself and his brother that was sufficiently important to determine which of them would continue in the family business:

[...] there were some personality issues and differences of opinion, and it was thought the best outcome was if we had a separation, which is what was organized. That was five or six years ago, and he [*the person who moved out*] is very successful, and the company has moved on. Again, whilst it is a difficult thing from the point of view of the family, it's not necessarily very much more difficult than any form of termination of employment – separation. Change is very traumatic no matter who you are. Taking the trauma out of separation is always a difficult thing to do. With a family it's a little bit more difficult – sometimes.

Once again we see the younger generation valuing the older generation's family values – but differently. The differences of opinion had a lot to do with the need to accept and foster change in the light of the needs of the business at its particular life cycle stage.

In none of the interviews did the CEOs specify exactly what had been their role in the termination of a family member's employment in the family business. For many the matter was obviously still painful and delicate, even though the CEO was confident the person who had left the business was now successful in their own right and everyone felt satisfied with the outcome. In all cases, the CEO's reasoning turned on the need to separate 'family' from 'business' on a temporary basis at least, and allow the issue to be resolved 'along business lines'. This is for the ultimate good of what all parties still see as a family business. As the CEO of the mountain resort business put it:

> **Respondent**: One of my main goals was to professionalize the business. They didn't have a chef when I went there. He called himself a chef, but he was an unqualified cook – who was married to the dining room supervisor who was a family-related cousin of [*name of the informant's uncle*] and his wife.
>
> **Interviewer**: A distant relation by marriage?
>
> **Respondent**: Yes. They were the first two that went actually. It's pretty hard to do anything with a place where the chef is not very good. So my goal was to bring in a professional management attitude, and to change the culture whereby only (blood-related members of the family) were allowed to make decisions.

A number of CEOs said such events were inevitable, given the numbers of people employed in the business and the greater intensity of feelings that arise when family members are involved. As with a number of other problems, clear communication is seen as the best solution:

[...] there have been times when family members have parted, and it's been shown to have been better from everybody's point of view that it happened. There's no right way of doing things. One person gets a job that the other feels that he should have got. The person who gets it might do it quite well, and the other person might have done it in a different way but also done it quite well. So it's better to have these things talked through. If necessary, assistance could be given to help the family member to go into some sort of business on his own, doing what he is good at. The big danger is in closing your eyes to it.

## Moving Outsiders In to the Family Firm

The opposite difficulty also occurs. As well as needing to move insiders out of the firm, most of the CEOs in our study, especially those in mature firms, had at some time dealt with the need to bring outsiders – professional staff who are not members of the family – in. Sometimes the two things need to be done at the same time. In that case the problem of separation is inverted: rather than achieving greater distance between people who once all were insiders, the distance between outsiders and insiders needs to be reduced.

To appreciate the practical implications of this problem, it helps to return to our definition of family business. In the first chapter we defined family business as being undertaken by blood-related members of the same family. Most of the CEOs in our study would have regarded people who had married blood relatives as members of the family, especially if they worked in the business. Even so, (and this is in line with our relatively narrow definition of family business outlined in Chapter 1), these relatives were not often seen as *expected* or *likely* to be part of the management structure of the business. In fact, some CEOs took it as accepted wisdom that in-laws should not and would not be part of the more important planning processes of the business. The following views were typical:

> [...] the wives are kept out of the business discussions, for obvious reasons. And that has helped too. I mean you can't start getting input from wives and in-laws etc. It just doesn't work.

> Everyone just accepts that it's the 'original' family and their descendants who form the core of the business; there are just too many sets of possibly conflicting interests if you start asking the others, by which I mean the in-laws.

Leon Danco takes a somewhat different view of the issue of bringing in in-laws into the firm. He would regard the attitudes expressed by these informants as unduly rigid and perhaps even counterproductive to the interests of the family business:

> **Leon Danco**: One of the main problems that we have seen in the States is one that when the daughter-in-law comes in, nobody bothers to explain the family dream. And so she sits there, doesn't understand what her husband is doing, doesn't understand where the business is going. All she knows is that's cash for her. And I think one of the main things in the States is the father-in-law has to take his daughter-in-law aside and explain what the dream was, how they got there, and why it makes her husband, the son, feel that the business is so special. And I think frequently the in-law children are left out and they end up causing all kinds of problems for the business.

Even if our business owners were to agree that in-laws should be kept better informed about the business, especially its 'dream', its values, they are unlikely to agree that in-laws should be closely involved with the strategic running of the business. Consider the case of the owner of the mountain resort firm. For him, bringing in 'outsiders', as he referred to his considerable numbers of professional, non-family staff, had been more difficult than moving insiders out. However this CEO – like others in the sample – was more willing to talk about what he had done to bring outsiders in than what he had needed to do to move insiders out. He described in detail the performance management systems he had introduced which would apply equally to members of the family and to 'outsiders'. Specifically, this CEO felt he needed to reduce the centralization of power in the family. In his view, this had encouraged 'politicking' which was adversely affecting the firm. The politicking did not come from the 'outside' staff, but from how members of the family themselves exerted a conscious or unconscious authority over the newcomers, stifling their ability to contribute to the firm. He described the instance of a capable 'outside' staff member whom the family had prevented from giving her best efforts to the firm. This was despite her abilities and her awareness of the problems the firm was facing:

> ... she [*a non-family member of the firm in a senior management position*] had a lot of talent, and is still doing very well. Here she was in this highly centralized structure, not so much a supervisor, but the manager of the resort, and she had no authority. She couldn't change jumpers without telling someone. So I could see that that was a big problem. She folded with the force, and became one of

those who just didn't worry. She just went along with the family member who would make the decision, or the one that would give you the pay rise.

In the end, it has been despite rather than because of the family influence in the management of the business that this CEO has been able to professionalize the firm. He has been bent on introducing appraisal systems, various forms of bonus pay and so on, during the period since he entered the firm. His success has been due to the 'outsiders' in his estimation, and the main problems have come from family members who have been used to other norms and practices:

> Looking at the process of change over the last five years, the only way to get through it is to have the support of the staff. The staff were one hundred per cent behind me, because I was looking at their interests, setting them up, giving them a career path, more responsibility, more wages, and giving them authority, and giving them training. The family wasn't greatly supportive of me at times, but the staff always were. So they have been a big help.

There is a further point to note about moving insiders out. In some cases in our research, friends of family members had held senior management positions in the business over many years. In the view of the person learning *our* business, they also became candidates for being moved outside when the need to professionalize the business became paramount. The CEO of a packaging firm in our study mentioned an example. His father, the founder of the business, had operated with the same managing director since shortly after the business began. As time passed, it became clear that the range of that person's skills was no longer sufficient to develop the business. As the present CEO put it:

> The managing director before me was M. He came up through the company and was appointed by my father mainly on the basis of his strengths in engineering and product development. The Peat Marwick report showed that we had a strong product development capacity, but the weak links were in the ability to develop the business.

> [...]

> The board was too introspective. My father [*the founder of the firm*] is also an inventor, and he and M. were more interested in sitting behind closed doors designing machinery, rather than talking about strategic issues, looking at the market, implementing management systems, etc. They weren't exactly stupid in terms of business acumen, but were more intuitive in their styles. And M. was

an authoritative person. This was suitable for the seventies, but today we look at trying to develop teams, and look for people skills. M. just didn't have the capability to do that.

There are both explicit and implicit life cycle issues here. The incumbent CEO's implied criticism of his predecessors' 'intuitive' learning styles suggests that prior, more formal learning and a wider experience beyond the firm is needed to help incumbent CEOs and the next generation move the family firm forward in terms of its next set of management priorities. In addition, this case makes it clear that the business and the family are closely entwined, as they will always be. This close link is behind the difficulties of keeping the business a family one – *our* business – yet also allowing it to professionalize and grow, move to a more developed stage of the firm life cycle. To do this, that is, to support the ideals and continuity of both the family and the firm, the current CEO felt he had had to act in ways that appeared to divide the family from the business. In his description of the issues and the actions surrounding his persuading M. to retire, this was very apparent:

**Respondent:** [*M.'s*] ability to run the company was one of the issues, and that did not relate to it being a family company. The problem was that getting rid of him, who was a very good friend of my father's over the last thirty-five years, while my father was chairman meant that my father was going against me. He was a director and told me that I would ruin the company. My father and I have been very close over many years. So I had to draw some lines between family and business.

**Interviewer:** How did you draw those lines?

**Respondent:** By being quite clearly focussed about the needs of this company. Where it needed to go, and what attributes were needed in its management. By being clear about the capabilities of the former managing director compared to what I could offer the company. All the shareholders and the people in the industry have seen what has happened in the transition from M. to myself and the current mood in the company is quite exciting.

While it is possible with hindsight to see the value of moving this person out, it had been difficult at the time. As the current CEO, who was a committed Christian, said:

From a Christian point of view it's sacrificing personal relationships for the business. But you have to act quickly and decisively, and then build those relationships again. And that's exactly what happened. In a month, through a process of getting back to my father and explaining what happened. I think secretly in this own heart he knew that something had to happen. You can't just continue on with no profits. He knew that the previous managing director wasn't performing, but he had put him into the job, and he was a long-time friend. But it had to be done. I knew it had to be done.

## Conclusion and Summary

In this chapter we saw that learners returning to the family firm after gaining experience outside it do something more than simply continue the kind of learning they did elsewhere. Working in the family firm entails learning *our* business. At first glance, we might think that this would be like coming to grips with the specific issues associated with any business, but there was more to it than that. Learning *our* business had to do with valuing the values of that business and the values of the people who had been – and generally still were – associated with creating it. Getting this right, that is, learning the values of that particular family business, ultimately prepares the learner for *leading* the family business. We will deal with this issue in our next chapter.

In revealing the shift in priorities between the practical implementation of the family business values at earlier and later times, the business life cycle helped draw out the particular issues that business was likely to be facing. However the learner had to reconcile how to deal with the business's shift in development to a later business life cycle stage with maintaining the values which were part of the fabric of the business. As a result, and as with the 'inside-outside' paradox of the previous chapter, our informants had to find ways to manage a paradox that seems peculiar to family businesses. They had to value certain values and continue them into the future, but also continue them *differently*.

We saw that there were two pathways through the 'continuing differently' paradox. Unlike the single, universal pathway 'go outside' which was the response to the 'inside-outside' paradox, both the pathways most of our respondents had followed in response to the 'continue differently' paradox were clearly influenced by the business life cycle. First, what our CEOs said about learning not just business but their *family* business, showed that the younger generation absorbs broad values and business philosophies from the older generation, but does not necessarily seek to emulate their previous strategies precisely. The skills or principles they absorb are general ones, such as having a cautious – but not timid – approach to debt. Perhaps it is failure to learn this 'strategic conservatism' that causes many family firms to begin to decline in their second generations. Nevertheless implementing these principles, including making decisions about the use of debt, varied according to what the CEO now saw as the new demands on the business created by its position on the life cycle curve.

The future CEO also had to learn about the market value of being a family firm. This was a complex pathway, and ways of following it were also influenced by the firm's stage on the life cycle curve. Simply being a family firm had market value in terms of customers and other firms seeing it as a closely-knit and stable entity. Many CEOs saw the importance of being part of that continuity, even when it was more a matter of perception than reality. Perceptions can be vital, however. The very perception that the business was family-based, sharing a common family culture and speedy processes of decision-making were valued by many CEOs – especially those contemplating growth, for example by extending their businesses to include joint ventures with overseas firms. Moreover, they often perceived the same values in family firms from other cultures, and this helped them establish the joint venture. This serves as a counterpoint to some other research on the internationalization of family business (see for example Davis, 1983; Gallo and Pont, 1996; Gallo and Sveen, 1991), which argues that the resistance of family businesses to outside information, and their tendency to concentrate on local markets, tend to inhibit their capacity to internationalize.

Some members of the younger generation in our study were well acquainted with the history and the organizational culture of their family's firm. While some theorists, for example Ward (1987), recommend this be done formally, our informants had generally done this in a natural, unforced way. Through knowing what others before them had believed to be important they had gained some forms of experience in a vicarious manner. They had also come to appreciate the founder's strategies, values and philosophies – and sometimes his or her errors – without incurring the emotional costs of a direct challenge to the founder.

The most obvious manifestation of the firm's movement along the life cycle curve is the CEO's interest in professionalizing the business. For this, the learner who is now approaching senior management or perhaps is already the CEO, sometimes had to move an insider out. That is he or she had to persuade a family member without the skills needed for the current stage in the firm's life cycle to leave the business. Sometimes the converse was necessary, that is, the new or aspiring leader had to know how to move an outsider in. Both of these are tasks that any business may need to cope with, but they have some special difficulties for the family business. This approach to 'continuing differently' involved gaining the support of everyone for this change, and moving people in or out in response to the demands of the business. The businesses in our study were seen as needing to become 'just like any other business' with formal control systems, performance appraisal and contingent rewards systems.

However even as the CEO tried to create a firm that was just like any other, he or she recognized this was always going to be something of an illusion. The family always remains an additional, complex factor that simplifies some issues yet complicates them at the same time. Here the value of being 'the same' in terms of the learner perceiving that he or she is choosing and continuing the values of a family business, conflicts with the need to be 'the same' as other businesses as they move upwards along the life cycle curve: professionally managed, technologically and competitively up to date, driven by hard data and proven skills. Managing the firm's movement along the life cycle curve looms still larger in the next chapter: 'Learning to *Lead* Our Business'.

## Note

[1] Leon Danco clarified later that his use of the word 'son' was meant to cover female members of the family as well as males. He was keen to point out that the times of the older son being the 'logical' successor even in preference to a more skilled daughter are over.

## References

Davis, John A. and Tagiuri, R. (1989), 'The Influence of Life Stage on Father-Son Work Relationships in Family Companies', *Family Business Review*, vol. 2, no. 1, Spring, pp. 47-74.

Davis, P. (1983), 'Realizing the potential of the family business', *Organizational Dynamics*, vol. 12, pp. 47-56.

Dunn, B. (1995), 'Success themes in Scottish family enterprises: Philosophies and practices through the generations', *Family Business Review*, vol. 3, no. 3, pp. 225-44.

Dunn, B. and Hughes, M. (1995), *Themes and issues in the recognition of family businesses in the UK*, paper presented to the Sixth European Family Business Network Conference, El Escorial, Madrid, September.

Gallo, M. and Pont, C. G. (1996), 'Important Factors in Family Business Internationalization', *Family Business Review*, vol. 9, no. 1, pp. 45-60.

Gallo, M. and Sveen, J. (1991), 'Internationalizing the family business: Facilitating and restraining factors', *Family Business Review*, vol. 4, no. 2, pp. 181-90.

McConaughy, D. (1994), *Founding family controlled corporations: An agency-theoretic analysis of corporate ownership structure and its impact upon corporate efficiency, value, and capital structure*, unpublished dissertation. Cincinnati, OH: University of Cincinnati.

McConaughy, D. and Phillips, G. Michael (1999), 'Founders versus Descendants: The Profitability, Efficiency, Growth Characteristics and Financing in Large, Public, Founding-Family-Controlled Firms', *Family Business Review*, vol. 12, no. 2, pp. 123-31.

Moores, K. and Mula, J. (1996), *Assessing 'Strategic Conservatism' of Australian Family Firms: An Examination of Strategies and Funding for Growth*, School of Business, Bond University, Gold Coast, Australia.

Poutziouris, P. Z. (2001), 'The Views of Family Companies on Venture Capital: Empirical Evidence from the UK Small to Medium-Size Enterprising Economy', *Family Business Review*, vol. 14, no. 3, pp. 277-91.

Ward, John L. (1987), *Keeping the Family Business Healthy: How to Plan for Continuing Growth, Profitability, and Family Leadership*, San Francisco, Jossey-Bass.

Yellow Pages (1995), *Small Business Index: A special report on small business growth aspirations and the role of exports*, Melbourne, Yellow Pages Australia, February.

# Chapter 5

# Learning to *Lead* Our Business

In the previous two chapters we discussed two major stages of what family businesses owners need to learn and how they learn it. We saw in Chapter 3 that the prospective CEO of the family business first had to learn the skills and attitudes needed for running a business *in general*. This typically involved leaving the family firm to gain general business experience elsewhere. As a consequence, it meant the family business had to deal with the particular paradox of that learning stage. We called it the 'inside-outside' paradox. It drew attention to the idea that leaving the family business, which is a necessary stage of learning the family business, is at the same time a threat to the survival of the family business, because the person leaving the business might not in fact return to it.

The prospective CEO next had to learn what was special about family business, that is, *our* business. By contrast with the first stage, learning *our* business typically meant returning to it, sometimes after a long period outside it. The learning priority for that learning stage was to understand and perpetuate the values associated with *our* business, the family business. There was also a new paradox to be managed during that stage. This paradox arose because, although the special values of the family business needed to be learnt and carried on, they generally had to be carried on *differently*.

The stage the family business had reached in its life cycle differed in the extent to which it shed light on the learning to be achieved in these two stages. In the first stage, learning business, it seemed to shed relatively little light on either the issues or their solutions. The future owner of the family business needed to go outside the business regardless of the stage the family business had reached. The specific location outside the business or the skill to be acquired might be influenced by the firm's life cycle stage, but the general pathway remains constant. By contrast, the life cycle stage the business had reached exerted seemed to clarify some aspects of the learning undertaken during the second learning stage. Typically, for example, the new generation had altered their interpretation of some values, such as the conservative use of debt, to reflect the more advanced stage of development the firm had reached.

In this chapter we move from learning about business and about *our* business, to learning about being *in charge* of the family owned business. Thus the next learning stage is learning to *lead* our business. This suggests some new questions: what is leadership and what might be special about how future owner managers of family businesses learn it? Much research has been done into different types or styles of leadership. But how do these relate to the stage the business has reached in its life cycle and how do they relate to family business?

Our approach to addressing these questions means that this chapter is a little different from the preceding ones. This is because it integrates quantitative data gathered about family firms with qualitative information derived principally from interviews. In particular we present information drawn from the perceptions of family business leaders (the CEOs) concerning leadership issues. How do they perceive their business contexts in terms of the sources of environmental uncertainty? What strategic choices do they make as responses to these uncertainties? In particular we identify the strategies, structures and systems of control that family firm leaders favour.

## The Nature of Leadership

Even with this very particular focus in our representation of the leadership problem, the very question 'what is leadership?' is a reminder that the nature of leadership is endlessly debated. It seems difficult to arrive at an agreed definition let alone an indication of which approaches to leadership are likely to enhance organizational effectiveness. Some researchers (for example, Miner, 1982) have even recommended a moratorium on leadership research until such matters are resolved. Some writers (for example, Foster, 1995) rely less on theory in defining what is needed to lead organizations including family businesses, citing 'sets of knowledge and skills' such as knowledge of the industry, technical and business skills, influence skills, and self-awareness as requirements for leadership. These are typically coupled with descriptions of specific 'learning strategies and situations' needed to acquire the skills, such as challenging assignments, ongoing feedback, learning from others, coursework and reading and self-directed learning (Foster, 1995, pp. 202-05).

Nevertheless, the field also continues to attract intense theoretical interest as researchers and business people alike remain intuitively convinced of leadership's importance to organizational life and its role in helping firms to be effective. Over time, researchers into organizational behaviour have moved from examining 'trait' approaches, which focus on particular attributes of leaders, to more sophisticated views which suggest that leadership styles should and do vary. While researchers have categorized types of leadership differently, some broad contrasting approaches consistently recur, such as the contrast between 'autocratic' and 'participative' approaches to leadership. A common assertion in the more recent leadership literature (see for example Bass, 1990; Bryman, 1999) is that the approach to leadership of organizations should be a contingent one, that is, that it needs to be adjusted to fit particular situations determined by various aspects of the business itself, the needs and talents of its staff and many other factors.

Still more recently, researchers including Bass (1990), Bass and Avolio (1990), and Bryman *et al.* (1996), have distinguished between 'transactional' and 'transformational' leadership approaches. According to a recent summary definition (Robbins, 2000), transactional leaders guide or motivate their followers in the direction of established goals by clarifying role and task requirements. Transformational leaders, by contrast, change followers' awareness of issues by helping them to look at old problems in new ways. They are able through their personal charisma and ability to stimulate their followers intellectually and even spiritually, to inspire followers to put out extra effort to achieve group goals. Theorists of transactional and transformational leadership are often at pains to stress that the two approaches are not really opposed, since both are necessary to getting things done. However, many also seem to stress that transformational leadership is superior to the transactional type (Bryman, 1999). Many researchers cite the importance of transformational leadership when major organizational change is needed (Bryman *et al.*, 1996).

Even if changes to major organizational goals are some time off, other, systems-related changes may happen sooner. The management literature has long studied how the entry of a new CEO acts as a catalyst for changes to management control systems in organizations (Miller, 1993). Others, have pointed to the link between CEO change and changes in accounting system choices (see, for example, Morrill and Waterhouse, 1994). The management and finance literatures have investigated the impact of the timing of a CEO change on accounting system design and financial performance (see, for example, Dalton and Kesner 1983, 1985; Sant, 1988). Miller identifies several changes that are typically expected to follow the appointment of a new leader: concentration of power, information processing systems, and organizational integration (Miller, 1993, p. 645). He proposed that most CEOs, because they are not as familiar as their predecessors with the practices and problems of their organizations, 'tend to look carefully at both their external environments and their internal operations to find out what is going on, especially before making key decisions' (Miller, 1993, p. 646).

Research indicates that the length of time CEOs have been in their position and whether they came from within or outside the firm affects firm performance, alters organizational systems, and brings about organizational change (Salancik and Pfeffer, 1980; Dalton and Kesner, 1983, 1985; Chung *et al.*, 1987; Lubatkin *et al.*, 1989; Miller, 1993; Datta and Guthrie, 1994; Morrill and Waterhouse, 1994). How the entry of the new CEO has been brought about, that is, the willingness or otherwise of the previous CEO to withdraw; CEO origin, that is, whether the CEO previously held a position within the firm or not; and CEO style, usually referred to as leadership or management style, all influence whether the CEO can be expected to instigate wide-ranging (transformational) or more narrowly based (transactional) change.

**Research on Leadership in Family Business**

In the context of family owned business, leadership research has not often dealt with the transactional/transformational distinction which has preoccupied much of the rest of the organizational behaviour field. Researchers have been more interested in differences in family owned business cultures and practices which are linked to – and in fact determined by – differences in leadership styles. For example, four broad leadership styles important in family business were discussed in a landmark study by Dyer (1986). More recently, Sorenson (2000), building on Dyer's work, distinguished five styles of leadership that seemed to be important in a large sample of family businesses located in Texas. Sorenson's five leadership styles in family business, summarized briefly, are as follows:

- *Participative leadership* The head of the family business involves organizational members in making decisions and guiding the organization, providing interpersonal processes for adaptation and change.

- *Autocratic leadership* By contrast with participative leadership, autocratic leaders are typically 'action-oriented' and 'doers', who tend to make decisions without consultation.
- *Laissez-faire/mission leadership* The laissez-faire approach to leadership allows freedom of choice in decision-making. It is generally assumed to have poor outcomes for the organization in terms of efficiency and productivity but, with the addition of boundary conditions established by the leader or the task itself (a 'mission'), can lead to productive and satisfied staff.
- *Expert leadership* This form of leadership derives from specialized knowledge and technical skill, that is, particular personal attributes of the leader.
- *Referent leadership* This form of leadership is also based on the leader's personal attributes, but this time, his or her capacity to inspire personal regard in others and a desire to please him or her.

Sorenson's research into family businesses suggests that these styles vary, sometimes in unexpected ways, in the extent to which they correlate with desired family and business outcomes such as high morale and low turnover. Only three of the styles appeared to be effective in providing desired outcomes. Specifically, referent leaders were able to exert interpersonal influence through modelling family values and showing insight about the business. Participative leaders relied on family values to guide behaviour, work openly and adaptively with the family business team, and consult with external experts. Laissez-faire/mission leaders, somewhat unexpectedly in Sorenson's view, also achieved desired outcomes through their use of organizational structure and planning to guide behaviour. However, only referent and participative leaders seemed to be able to produce outcomes that were desirable for both the family *and* the business.

## Learning Priority – Perspicacity

In this chapter, we will draw together some of these findings about leadership in family business, but with some additional insights from our own research. Just as in the previous learning stages, we can expect there to be a number of paradoxes and conflicts in this 'learning leadership' stage since, as before, the family and the business need to be made to work together. Leading the family business – now as always – involves not impeding its family nature. In fact the family nature of the firm should actually enhance the way the firm meets its goals. As a result, leading the family business becomes a special case of the problem of leadership which is increasingly seen as being not merely a matter of style, but as a question of ideas and values.

We have seen from earlier chapters that ideas for leading family business are gained outside the business and by constantly scanning the environment. Values, by contrast, are learned inside the business from the family itself and by applying knowledge gained outside to the special situation and peculiar qualities of the family business. This of course is no small task. So what are the qualities of perspicacity or insight on the part of the leader are required to bring these two systems – family and business – together for the benefit of both?

In addition, and in line with our focus in earlier chapters, we are interested to see how leadership in family business is associated with the stages of the organizational life cycle. Judging the needs of the business in terms of the business life cycle also requires qualities of perspicacity. The changes in development denoted by the business life cycle suggest that the transactional/transformational distinction is likely to be relevant to family business just as it is to others. Consistent with the more general literature on transactional and transformational leadership, it seems likely that transactional leadership in family business will be appropriate for handling the transactions relevant to the current stage of the organizational life cycle. Transformational approaches, on the other hand, could be expected to be needed if the leader of the family business judges that he or she needs to guide it through a transition to a later, more developed stage on the life cycle curve.

## Control and Leadership of Family Business

Returning to our research definition of family business provides a way of approaching both these leadership issues: first, leading the family firm so that family and business work together in mutually enhancing ways; second, leading the family firm in relation to its life cycle, that is, handling its transactions within the current stage of the life cycle or transforming it through a later stage. As we saw in Chapter 1, even allowing for some variety of definition, family businesses are those *controlled* by a family, whether through family ownership of shares, presence of family members on the board or by the dominance of family members in the general management of the businesses. The last of these is the most common even if elements of control through share ownership and governance structures co-exist.

Given the importance of family control to family business, it is helpful to recall that both the organizational life cycle and the various classifications of organizational strategy have been seen as ways of broadly differentiating, of 'framing' various forms of control – in the sense of how managers of organizations seek to respond to different sources of environmental uncertainty. Control systems, we saw in Chapter 2, are part of managers' efforts both to set goals for their organizations and to assess the organization's progress towards them. Control systems in family business, researchers often noted, often seemed to emphasize clan or culturally based controls more so than more formal, accounting-based approaches to ensuring that organizational directions were set and targets met.

Seen in the context of these directional or goal-setting issues, control is a vital feature of the leadership task. It is virtually a cliché to point out that leaders provide vision and direction for their organizations, and that when their organizations deviate from what are seen as the best paths towards their goals, it is the leader's job to return the organization to its proper course. Leaders of family owned business, then, are also concerned with these issues of setting and achieving goals, and they deal with these issues within a family context as well as a business one. Of course, the second stage of learning – learning *our* business – meant gaining an understanding of what was special about family business. Once the learner reaches the leadership stage, however, more is required than an ability to appreciate and put to use the special qualities of the family business. The leader needs to do this, but also to guide the response of the family business so as to optimize its position in relation to the broader business environment. Let us try to bring all the issues into focus. We can say that the special task of the CEO of the family business is defined by the need to control the internal responses of the family business organization in relation to the uncertainties provided by its internal and external context, including the context of its family nature.

## Researching Family Business Control Responses

Our research, based on surveys and interviews with family business CEOs in Australia, provides insights into what these CEOs perceive as the major sources of uncertainties confronting their firms, and how they respond to these in terms of the strategic choices that affect the structures and systems within their firms. Our research is thus a means of coming to grips with some specific issues of the control – and thus the leadership – of successful family owned businesses. As noted in Chapter 2, the research adopted a contingency perspective in associating life cycle stages with the design and uses of a successful control system. We report our findings about the life cycle issues in Chapter 7.

To gather data for the research questions, we used both a mailed questionnaire and follow-up detailed interviews with selected respondents. The questionnaire asked about key areas known to affect the success of business management: the uncertainties of the business environment, strategies, structure and control systems. A statistical technique known as factor analysis was used to reduce the detail of the questions, and also to confirm underlying dimensions found in studies of non-family business. Then, we used correlation analysis to see which aspects of the key areas above seemed to drive the form and content of the firm's control systems.

The finer detail of the survey methods used to collect the data, and the types of analysis undertaken are contained in the Appendix. At this point, however, it is important to note that filtering techniques were incorporated into the questionnaire to ensure, first, that non-family firms were not included in the group whose responses were analysed and, second, that only successful family firms were being examined. For our purposes 'successful' firms were defined as those that had been in existence for no less than five years and were being run by the second generation of a single family. They thus had survived the entrepreneurial stage of the founder.

## Specific Issues

Let us now examine how the study tapped into the leadership issues we are concerned with. The study investigated:

- family firms' perceived levels *environmental uncertainty* (the firms' external context),
- the responses of family businesses to their environments, in terms of *strategy* and *structure* (the firms' internal context), and
- the characteristics of family firms' *control systems*.

Figure 5.1 sets out the contingency factors in our research design to show the relationship between various leadership issues we investigated.

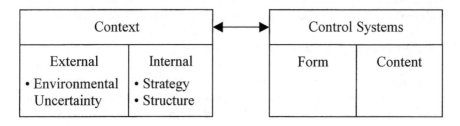

**Figure 5.1     Research design**

For each of the issues of environmental uncertainty, strategy, structure and control systems, we present here a summary view of how concerned the leaders of family firms were about them. For each of these issues we also present the results of *factor analyses* to show which general ideas or dimensions seemed to underlie these issues for CEOs of family owned businesses. Finally in this chapter we will briefly present the results of *correlation analyses* to show which of the dimensions underlying the four issues – environmental uncertainty, strategy and structure – seemed to drive the control systems that family business owners use to lead their firms. In Chapter 7, where we present the profiles of successful family businesses, we will extend this analysis to relate perceptions about the environment, and the use of strategies, structures and control systems in the family firm to the stages of the firm life cycle. We present the general results of our quantitative analyses of these four issues here. More detail, including tables, is presented in the Appendix.

*Environmental Uncertainty*

In this part of the study CEOs reported their perceptions of the competitive intensity of their industry in terms of customers, competitors, and levels of innovation and competition. The overall mean response showed that family businesses experience a moderate level of uncertainty in their environments. However the increase in legal, political, and economic constraints surrounding firms and the intensity of price competition dominated as sources of uncertainty for leaders of family firms. Owners of family businesses in our study regarded price competition as a prime source of uncertainty. At least there was some relative stability to be gained through human resources, which our CEOs did not see as being subject to large amounts of competition. Similarly, for the businesses in our study, the frequency of technological discoveries did not seem to present major problems.

## Dimensions of Environmental Uncertainty

When these results were analysed for their underlying dimensions, it appeared that family business owners perceive the nature of environmental uncertainty to consist mainly of two broad issues: change and complexity. They see the dynamics of change largely in terms of technological changes arising from the frequency of scientific discoveries in their industry and the extent of economic stability or otherwise arising from these discoveries. This dimension we labelled *Technoeconomic* factors. By contrast, complexity is associated with the intensity of competition for both inputs and outputs, as well as the increase in legal, political and economic constraints on their firms. This second dimension was labelled *Competition and constraints.*

Further, quantitative information about *Environmental Uncertainty* and its underlying dimensions is presented in Tables A.1 and A.2 of the Appendix.

## Internal Responses – Strategies and Structures

As we pointed out earlier, the strategies and structures leaders of family firms adopt are part of their internal responses to environmental uncertainty. Let us consider first strategies and then structures in terms of how they were used by leaders of family firms in our sample, and then the underlying dimensions of each of them.

## Strategies

In the strategy questions, our CEOs were invited to describe the explicit strategies their firms pursued. The questions covered products, company expansion, marketing, placing an emphasis on quality, and the use of external advisers. The overall mean results suggest that family firms only make modest use of explicit strategies. Some strategies were not employed at all by some businesses.

## *Dimensions of Strategies*

In the same way as we did for the family business leaders' perceptions of the underlying sources of uncertainty in their environments, we analysed their responses about strategies to see if there were any patterns underlying them. The results showed that family business owners seemed to view their strategic options as belonging to three broad categories: *product differentiation, diversification,* and *marketing* alternatives.

- *Product differentiation* Product differentiation, which included making sure the family firm was the leader in new product introduction and market segmentation, using prestige pricing and advertising, dominating distribution channels, and having different products are all aspects of product differentiation strategies. The product differentiation group of strategies was the dominant one selected by leaders of family businesses in our study.
- *Diversification strategies* Family business owners perceive another group of strategies as related to diversification, whether internal or external, expanding geographically or integration, whether upwards or downwards. However in contrast to product differentiation, while family business owners recognize these measures as a class of strategic options, they tend not to be used by family owned businesses.
- *Marketing strategies* The remaining strategies are somewhat diverse, but nevertheless, considered together, they suggest some notion of *marketing* strategies. Accordingly, we grouped the remaining strategies, which include frequent product innovations, price cutting, cooperation with competitors and the risk attitude of senior managers into a broad, *marketing* strategies group. Again, this is not a group of strategies which family business owners tend to favour.

Further, quantitative information about *Strategies* and their underlying dimensions is presented in Tables A.3 and A.4 of the Appendix.

## *Structure*

We asked owners of family businesses questions to measure the degrees of delegation, divisionalization and formalization operating in family businesses. The overall average of their responses again suggests that leaders of family firms employ modest levels of structure. There was little variation across all questions. In common with many other categories of firms there is a low level of delegation of authority for the selection of large investments. However the extent to which the firm's operations are grouped around specific products or services suggests that activities in this area are fairly highly structured.

*Dimensions of Structure*

When we analysed the raw results to see what family business owners regard as the underlying dimensions of business structure, we found two broad factors. Family business owners see the issue of structuring their firms in terms of, first, the *Structure of Authority* and, secondly, the *Structure of Activities.* That is, family business owners see overall structure as formed by the broad issues of the reporting structure of the firm, and the ways tasks are organized.

Further, quantitative information about *Structure* and its underlying dimensions is presented in Tables A.5 and A.6 of the Appendix.

*Control Systems*

In trying to understand how leaders of family business use control systems, we assessed them in terms of two aspects: their content and their form. In respect of 'content' issues, we asked about the extent to which a range of mainly financial controls were used in the management of family businesses. The importance of such controls from balance sheets to budgets was measured along with the frequency of formal directors or partners meetings and the types of training programs in place. The 'form' questions asked family business leaders to indicate the importance of the scope, focus, quantification, and timeliness of information to the firm when making decisions.

The aspects that dominated the 'content' of control systems in family business were the use of computerized systems, the preparation of monthly profit and loss statements and the control of cash by preparation of cashflow statements. By contrast, less used 'content' controls included manual systems of accounting, the use of total quality techniques like Just in Time (JIT), Materials Resources Planning (MRP), and Quality Circles, comparing the firm with industry averages, internal auditing, calculating internal rates of return for evaluating investments, external auditing firms, the frequency of formal directors' meetings and systematic performance of managerial staff using budgets and long term planning and forecasting of sales and profits. See Table A.7 for quantitative detail about the 'content' of control systems in family firms.

The results for the 'form' questions about control systems yielded a moderately high mean score, showing that the speed of delivery of a diverse range of information was relatively important. Leaders of family businesses clearly value having only a short delay between when an important event happens and when they get relevant information about it. In fact, the responses on all the questions were skewed towards the higher end of the scale indicating that family businesses tend to value information that is broadly based and supplied quickly. See Table A.9 for quantitative detail about the 'form' of family business control systems.

## Content Dimensions in Control Systems

When we analysed the results of the 'content' questions to determine whether we could find underlying patterns, we found five broad dimensions, as follows:

- *Management Controls* The first factor, which we labelled 'management controls', was dominated by questions relating to the establishment of profit and cost centres and the associated profit targets and cost controls. It also included performance evaluation of managers and their participation in budget preparation. This factor was easily the most important of the five to our family business owners.
- *Operational Controls* Operational controls formed a second factor. This was dominated by the control of inventories, the scheduling of operations and the control of operations by techniques such as Just in Time (JIT), Materials Resources Planning (MRP) and Quality Circles. Cost control of operations, internal auditing and the use of internal rates of return (IRR) calculations to control asset acquisitions were other forms of operational controls.
- *Financial Reporting* The third factor to emerge was one in which the controls were conventional financial reports. The use of monthly balance sheets, profit and loss statement, and cashflow statements were the basis of this factor which we labelled 'financial reporting'.
- *Accounting Systems* and *External Controls* These two factors were neither as reliable nor as significant as the first three factors.

Further information is given in Table A.8 of the Appendix.

*Form Dimensions of Control Systems*

In terms of underlying factors, the 'form' questions coalesced into two reliable factors. The first factor, which we called *Scope of Information*, was dominated by characteristics relating to the quantification, futurity, non-financial, and externally oriented nature of information. The second factor related exclusively to a time dimension with the frequency of reporting and the delays in receiving information loading strongly, so we labelled this *Timeliness of Information*. Further information is given in Table A.10 of the Appendix.

## What Drives Control Systems in Family Firms?

So far, our analysis aimed to uncover the broad dimensions that leaders of family businesses perceived as underlying the issues of environmental uncertainty, strategy, structure and control systems in successful family firms, and the extent to which they were concerned with such issues. After this, we used a technique known as correlation analysis to try to see how these underlying dimensions relate to each other. Correlation coefficients indicate the degree to which change in one dimension is related to change in another. They not only summarize the strength of association between a pair of dimensions, but also provide a way of comparing the strength of relationship between one pair of dimensions and another pair. In particular, given our interest in leadership and control of family firms, we wanted to know what was driving the form and content of the control systems. Was it an external driver such as the prevailing levels of environmental uncertainty? Alternatively, was it internal influences emanating from the strategy and structure of the business? Furthermore, we needed to consider whether the *interrelationship* of firm strategy and structure could also influence the nature of control systems.

We carried out our correlation analysis in two stages. First, we looked for simple correlations among the factors underlying environmental uncertainty, structure, strategy, and the content and form of control systems. Second, partial correlations among the variables taken two at a time and controlling for all others were determined. This would allow us to see whether a single variable might be driving the relationship. Again, we present the results in general terms here. The detail of our quantitative analyses is presented in the Appendix; see Tables A.11 and A.12.

## Coping with the External Environment

Our results showed that environmental uncertainty is only moderately associated with either the content or form of control systems in successful family firms. In fact it is only the *Technoeconomic* dimension that is related to one of the 'content' aspects (*Accounting Systems*) and both 'form' aspects: *Scope* and *Timeliness*. This suggests that in successful family firm high levels of uncertainty arising from a changing technoeconomic situation are accompanied by increased computerization of accounting systems and the provision of information of broader scope, supplied in a timely fashion.

## Coping with the Internal Environment

However the correlations tell a different story when we consider aspects of the internal environment of family firms. Both structural and strategic factors are significantly associated with the major content and form dimensions of control systems. Both the *Structure of Authority* and the *Structure of Activities* have highly significant associations with *Management Controls*. These positive correlations indicate that as leaders of family firms make more use of delegation and establish departments and divisions, they also use more sophisticated management controls. In particular, as departments and divisions are established, family businesses begin assigning cost and profit centre financial responsibilities to managers. Such financial responsibilities are reinforced through greater emphasis on managerial performance evaluation and the active participation of managers in budget preparation. While the statistical results of our study do not allow us to say so for sure, it is possible that these structural and systems changes are introduced together as a package of internally consistent controls. This is consistent with the interview evidence which we will consider later in this chapter, and also with other studies.

Moreover, *Operational Controls* are also positively related to both *Structure of Authority* and *Structure of Activities*. Thus more sophisticated forms of operational control also coincide with increased levels of delegation and divisionalization. Controlling inventories and scheduling operations in particular, together with other quality techniques were ways family firms reinforced the control of operations in the face of structural change. Other financially oriented controls used to moderate extents in the control of operations were standard costs, internal rate of return (IRR) calculations and internal auditing.

## Strategies and Control

Two of the *Strategies* dimensions are also associated with increased levels of sophistication in management controls. An emphasis on *Product Differentiation* and *Diversification* strategies coincides with the development of cost and profit centres along with increased levels of management participation in budget preparation. However there is less emphasis upon these budgets in how managers are later evaluated. This indicates that leaders of family businesses may use budgets more as a means of forecasting than as features of any management control system.

## Structures and Control

Both the structural factors are significantly positively associated with the two 'form' dimensions of control systems. The *Structuring of Authority* and *Structuring of Activities* are positively associated with the *Scope of Information* and the *Timeliness of Information*. *Strategies* however are only associated with the *Scope of Information* and not its speed of delivery (*Timeliness*). In particular, firms with a product differentiation orientation value non-economic information such as customer preferences, employee attitudes, labour relations and the attitudes of governments and consumer organizations. Information about broad external factors such as economic conditions, population growth and technological developments together with historical information that relates to possible future events also supported the *Product Differentiation* strategies of family owned businesses.

The broader *Scope* and increased *Timeliness of Information* tend to reinforce the *Management* and *Operational Controls* rather than any of the other aspects of the formal control systems. These features are associated more with internal controls that may well be less formally organized.

CEOs of family firms also saw some other factors than those relating to control systems as being related. *Technoeconomic* uncertainty arising from technological discoveries and the economic change caused by the introduction of products was associated with *Product Differentiation* and *Marketing* strategies as well as the way *Activities* were structured. Interestingly however, the *Competition and Constraints* factor was not significantly associated with any strategic, structural or systems factors.

That is, despite the fact that leaders of family firms seemed to be in strong agreement on some dimensions of this factor (for example, its level of intensity), they have yet to identify appropriate ways of dealing with these externally induced uncertainties. No strategic, structural or systems level responses appear to accompany family business CEOs' realization of how external constraints and competition affect their firms.

This analysis implies that firm structures and strategies, that is, the internal environment of the family firm, is more strongly positively associated with the characteristics of the systems leaders use to control them than the external uncertainties. These results could, however, arise from the relationships *between* firm strategies and structures. To investigate whether these structural and strategy factors drive the development of family business control systems in their own right, we used partial correlation analysis.

**Partial Correlation Analysis**

Partial correlation analysis allowed us to determine if any one of the dimensions we had discerned as underlying the issues of environmental uncertainty, strategy and structure, were driving any of the correlations noted above. To this end, the variables are taken two at a time controlling for all others.

Our results show that both aspects of *Structure* (*Structure of Authority* and *Structure of Activities*) and, to lesser extents, *Strategies* and *Environmental Uncertainty* influence both the 'content' and 'form' of controls. By far it is the *Management Controls* and *Operational Controls* of family firms that are most strongly associated with these factors. Both the *Structuring of Authority* and *Activities* along with the pursuit of *Diversification* strategies are all highly positively associated with the development of sophisticated management controls. However, *Operational controls* are not driven by *Diversification* strategies but are rather, albeit to a lesser extent, by *Marketing* strategies. *Authority Structures* and the *Structuring of Activities* both significantly drive *Operational Controls*.

The sophistication of *Financial Reporting* tends to be driven by the *Structuring of Activities* and *Diversification* strategies and to a far lesser extent by the level of *Competition and Constraints* prevailing in the external environment and the family business's internal *Structure of Authority*. The development of computerized accounting systems is, interestingly, driven largely by an internal feature, the *Structuring of*

*Authority.* Lesser drivers for such systems include internal *Structuring of Activities* and external *Technoeconomic* uncertainties.

Concerning the form of information supplied, it is only a *Product Differentiation* strategy that drives the increasing breadth of *Scope of Information*. Leaders of family firms which pursue product differentiation strategies would appear to value broad historical information external to their firm such as economic conditions, population growth and technological developments, together with other non-economic information especially if it relates to possible future events.

The partial correlation analysis tends to confirm that firm structures and strategies, that is, the internal environment, drives the sophistication of controls employed by family firms. These factors impact most heavily on the management and operational controls used.

## Foreshadowing the Learning Tasks of Family Firm Leadership

From our analysis so far, we can be confident that factors in the internal rather than the external environment drive the growth in sophistication of control systems in family firms. We have also seen that, among these internal factors, clusters of issues rather than a single factor appears to drive one drives this development. Yet the picture yielded by the linkages between factors in the external and internal environment and the development of control and management systems still appears complex. Are there ways we – and leaders of family firms – might discern patterns in these findings? For example, in the picture of controls we have produced so far, how might we link clan or social-type controls to the broad task of setting and monitoring goals related to the broad thrust of the business? By contrast, how might we determine where market and bureaucratic, accounting-based output controls might be more appropriate? In our discussion of agency theory in Chapter 2, we posited, along with Schulze *et al.* (2001) that the simple fact of being a family firm was not itself a guarantee of success, or even that there will necessarily be special efficiencies derived from reductions in agency costs. So how might we determine where and how different types of control will be associated with firm survival and growth? These issues are no less than the learning tasks of leadership itself, in terms of the leader's role in addressing the firm's external and internal sources of uncertainty.

We will return to these issues in our quantitative analysis in Chapter 7 when we further analyze CEOs' perceptions of their firms. At that point we will consider the firms not only in terms of these individual context and control factors and the specific linkages between them, but in terms of what the *patterns* in these linkages suggest about the firms' positions on the business life cycle curve. That is we will consider the patterns of factor linkages in conjunction with our classifications of the firms in our sample as Stage 2 or *Collectivity* firms, Stage 3 or *Formalization and Control* firms, or Stage 4, *Elaboration of Structure* firms. We will consider, for example, whether clan controls indeed play a dominant role in the control of Stage 2 *Collectivity* firms, more so than they do in Stage 3 or 4 firms. We will examine whether, as firms develop from collectivities, clan-type traditions give way to more institutionalized procedures resulting from the formalization of management practices, and whether this is accompanied by a move somewhat away from clan controls and towards greater salience of bureaucratic and market controls.

### Systems in Family Owned Firms – The Interview Evidence

Now we are ready to look more closely at what our interview evidence says about the kinds of systems exercised by leaders of family owned businesses and how they developed these different approaches. The quantitative analysis has already shown that, by contrast with the earlier learning stages, there was no single pathway or limited set of pathways that somehow could be taken as 'solving' the issue of how to lead the family firm. 'Learning business' required virtually a single pathway – leaving the firm, sometimes for long periods. 'Learning *our* business' involved a limited set of specific and consistent pathways through the paradox of 'continuing differently': adopting broad strategies rather than the detail of the previous generation's practices, and learning the market value of family business. By contrast, learning to *lead* the family firm is much more complex. The analysis we have just undertaken gives an inkling of the issues to be dealt with. Learning leadership seems to impose the requirement of *perspicacity* – the need for the CEO to be able to work out how to respond to the demands of various kinds of environmental uncertainty, whether internal or external.

Yet some broad approaches seem to be possible, leading to some consistent profiles of success. In Chapter 7 we will return to our quantitative analysis to consider how the stage family businesses in our sample had reached in the business life cycle illuminates some of the patterns and profiles of success in dealing with the complexities of family business leadership. For the moment, however, let us consider what our respondents had to say about how they arrived at their practical approaches for managing the problems of leading the family business.

## The Paradox of Leading Family Businesses – 'Informal Formality'

From the interview evidence, achieving the perspicacity or insight needed to lead the family firm often seems to centre on knowing how to use apparently contradictory approaches to management control at the same time. The quantitative evidence showed the internal environment was influencing CEOs' approaches to developing systems in family owned businesses more than external uncertainties. Paralleling this, in the interviews, we often saw evidence of 'informal formality' in how family firms were run, that is, formal and informal controls being exercised together.

*Systems and Intuition*

In the case of one firm we examined extensively, the owner emphasized the quality and extent of the systems he had instigated, but nonetheless had to concede that at least some of his success had to do with less formal, intangible personal qualities of insight into the market that suggested he undertake a new venture far from the business's original base in South Australia. Rather than anything which his systems could have led him to predict, he had an intuitive, 'second-guessing' capacity which meant he could work out where the market would move in the future.

> I was something of the 'prodigal son'. Our business in South Australia was strong. We were growing; the eastern seaboard was a market place where we had low market share. We had good market knowledge, good people, we knew there were no local manufacturers of our types of products in Queensland; they were all being supplied out of Adelaide, Sydney or Melbourne. Back in 1975, Queensland was not the flavour of the month ... [*but rather*] the backwater of the world. It was not the place to be, but we thought it was, and we established our business when things were quiet, and when things started to grow, we grew the business substantially.

*Formalization and 'Clan' Controls*

Another frequently mentioned aspect of the practical qualities of leadership was the ability to create a sense of loyalty in family and outside staff alike.

This was not done in a blind way, but by creating the potential for a genuine merging of staff interests and the interests of the firm. This loyalty went beyond family members and in fact the CEOs did not see it as trying to make non-family members feel the same as family. Rather, the CEO felt that his or her strength lay in being able to create a sense of purpose that both built on and transcended immediate family bonds. From the owner of a large party hire business:

> I think that I have been able to attract and obtain loyalty from some very good people. We have been able to take advantage of the strengths of the family business, perhaps more so than some of our competitors where there's change of management regularly.

Leaders of family firms seemed to be intuitively aware, along with Hopwood, Ouchi and other researchers we cited in Chapter 2, that clan or social type controls had a major role to play in family firms. They worked hard to ensure that the high levels of trust between family members were used both in ensuring healthy family relationships *and* in determining the broad thrust of the business. However more conventional, accounting-based output controls were considered appropriate for day-to-day operational aspects of the family business, particularly when leaders were dealing with 'outsiders' or when they judged it was time to 'professionalize' the business. It seems that for many family business owners this uniting of the two approaches to control was the most effective way of achieving both management control of the firm and harmony between the family and the business elements of the firm. We might also see it as a pragmatic uniting of transactional and transformational approaches to leadership, since it so often accompanied managing the day-to-day issues of running the firm at the same time as attempting to professionalize it and take it to a further, more developed stage of the business life cycle.

*Balancing Formality and Informality – The Challenge of Growth*

As we might imagine, tasks such as leading family and non-family members of the firm, being both a transactional and a transformational leader are not easy, particularly when decisions about change needed to be confronted. Growth was one of the forms of change that informants in our sample frequently faced. With growth the leader recognized the need for a more professionalized approach to particular staff issues, such as the greater formality of job roles. This corresponds to more formal kinds of control such as Child's centralized personal controls and Ouchi's bureaucratic controls we discussed in Chapter 2. Both of them differ from the informal kinds of control which characterized the family business before the change. Adopting these 'formal' kinds of control means accepting that not all employees within a business are equal. This runs counter to the idea that siblings are entitled to equal rights. As one informant said, in the course of a discussion about the need for formal job descriptions and performance-based bonuses:

> But it's a thing you really need to do if you want to professionalize your business and make it grow. What we find as the third generation is that if there is an issue of bonuses, or role descriptions or an issue of this nature, the third generation people can be very critical of each other – in a constructive way of course. But the parents can't. They've spent their whole life trying to treat their children as equally as possible, and to bring them in to a business situation where you say that you have to give something to this one and not to that one, they can't do it.

The tension between the values of 'family' and the need to vary the old informal approaches to respond to change appeared again when another informant discussed a possible move into export markets. This potential for growth meant the family influence might be reduced or even eliminated:

> We now will have to decide: do we continue to grow? And that will bring with it certain questions such as how are we going to finance it, do we go to the market for more capital etc. Then those have flow-on questions. If we do that, does the family lose control? Is it going to be no longer a family company? Will it fall into the hands of foreign owners as so many companies have?

Maintaining control in these more complex situations demands more information and more information means a need for more formal and complex ways of providing it. As we saw from our quantitative analysis, the use of computerized systems, the preparation of monthly profit and loss statements, and the control of cash by preparation of cashflow statements come to dominate management control systems in successful family businesses. The use of manual systems of accounting in our sample of firms was less prevalent.

Yet within these more formal approaches to control, the value of less formal controls remains high. Leaders need to be 'formally informal' or 'informally formal'. This 'informal formality' paradox is illustrated by one family firm leader's approach to introducing a professional approach to performance appraisal. A formal performance appraisal scheme was introduced when a number of outside staff joined the firm. However the CEO wished to use the system to evaluate family members' performance as well. As he recognized, at one level formal performance appraisal runs counter to the 'clan' or family norms of trust, and could not be introduced in one move, or in a heavy-handed way. He said he had achieved this change and a number of others 'by stealth'.

> I didn't come in as the boss. I took up a position in the firm when the other manager was still there. It was more a matter of the way things were done. Getting them [*the other members of the firm*] to have a regular meeting, and having a system of reviewing performance of people, setting out job descriptions, giving people authority, and things like that.

Despite this surreptitious approach to introducing more formal controls, the former CEO of this firm, that is, the father of the person we quoted above, told us there is no mistaking the authority that the current leader held from the moment he took over.

> **Interviewer**: So he's the boss, and he acts like one?
>
> **Respondent [*father of the current CEO*]**: Yes he's the general manager now, and he's very capable. With the staff, some say he's abrupt, but you've got to be. He's not a good person for the front office, for reception, because he's a bit too abrupt, but behind the scenes, running the place, he's so good.

and later:

> **Respondent**: Without a doubt, S. [*name of the present CEO*] is the boss. He has much more experience. [...] There's no family conflict at all, and you've got to have one person at the head. S. has the brains, and knows what it's all about.

The same informants stressed that others in the firm also need to know their areas of responsibility more clearly than in the past. Despite this, the former CEO and even the present one, who had brought in the changes, recalled with nostalgia the time when 'we didn't have to sit around a board room' and when a rough and ready division of jurisdiction between him and his brother – the original leaders of the firm – had been enough to run the business.

> **Interviewee [*father of the current CEO*]**: I was inside and he was outside. The roles were well defined. I did the hiring and firing and the ordering – anything

to do with 'internal'. P. [*his brother, and a co-founder of the firm*] did the guest activities and other projects. No doubt he was inside as well, but the main theme was that I did the inside and he did the outside.

## The Board of Directors as a Source of Insight

Another way in which leaders achieve perspicacity or insight as the firm moves upward on the organizational life cycle curve is to make greater use of formal control through directors' meetings. In the sample of businesses where we interviewed CEOs and others, each business had a formal board of directors, although there were variations in the board's composition and how frequently and formally the board met. Second, whatever the size and composition of the board, decision-making mechanisms and areas of responsibility tended to be clearer now than they were earlier. Even with the operations of the board, a kind of 'informal formality' tends to be maintained, as one leader in our sample pointed out when discussing the change he had made to push the firm in a more market-oriented direction:

> One of the changes [*associated with firm's move towards a greater market focus*] was to change the board structure. We have never operated an efficient board, and may never do so in fact. We have a conflict between the roles of the board and the roles of the senior management team. For example, the board spends a large proportion of its time monitoring the performance of the senior management, when the senior management is spending a lot of time monitoring its own performance and the performance of the business – an obvious duplication. Also a lack of ability by the board to think strategically – a lot of strategic decisions are being made by the management.

Even though the problems of an inefficient board are obvious, researchers on the topic (for example Schwartz and Barnes, 1991) strongly support their creation, and recommend that they include more rather than fewer outside members. For them to work well, CEOs need to want a board with outside members, members need to have been selected carefully, and outsiders need to understand the board's expectations of them. The CEO in this example is reluctant to change the board to make it more formal and efficient. Nevertheless, most of our informants favoured regular meetings of the boards of directors as the firm grew, and required that the boards include outsiders. This was sometimes as a way of *countering* the forms of control exercised by the family, which were sometimes judged by family firm leaders to have the potential to create resistance to necessary change aimed at professionalizing the firm. One CEO spoke about the value of a particular outside director in these terms:

> R. [*name of an outside, non-executive director on the board of his firm*] is coming to see that the influence of outsiders on the board is important. I can see it quite plainly. R. sees what seem to be small matters come to the board meeting. They seem to be unimportant, almost routine, and he is surprised that they even get onto the board agenda. Then, at the meeting, his impression seems to be confirmed by the fact that they get passed through easily. What he doesn't see that this is partly because of his presence there. He doesn't understand that if he wasn't there, the matters might not be simple. Family issues would probably come in more. So I'm working bit by bit to try to change the board, and bring more outsiders on.

Leon Danco has an even more telling example of the ways leaders of family businesses need to work with family members to make the most of the values of trust which simplify many control issues in family businesses and yet can be the source of disruption to the introduction of more formal approaches to control by the family business leader. He cites the following case from his experience as a consultant:

> **Leon Danco**: I worked with a family business one time where the person being trained to take over the family business was the son, but he had a number of older sisters. Now the son had done everything necessary – got himself a good education, got experience in another business – he seems to be pretty good. But one of the older daughters was a problem. Without knowing it, perhaps, she took great pains to upset the succession process. You see, she was twelve years senior to her only brother. As she was around twelve when he was born, she changed his nappies, and she mothered him because her mother had all these other children to cook for and clean and run the house. So she was this little guy's mother for four years of his life. Now all of a sudden, he is thirty something and she is forty-two, forty-three, or forty-four or thereabouts, and she still thinks that she can mother him. And he still thinks that he is the son. And sometimes you will have multiple kids that go through this process – and none of them can become the family business leader because of the view of them that the others have. The acceptance by the family of the leadership of the child is essential. ...

Leon Danco also speaks about the importance of creating a measurable track record that both the board and the family will recognize as evidence that the person who has been learning to lead the family business has in fact learnt enough to take over the leadership role:

**Leon Danco**: Dad has to allow the creation or to create job opportunities where you can show off, whether it's opening up a branch elsewhere, running a new department, taking care of a new product, where wins or loses is entirely on the son's ability. There are a whole group of people who take money from their business, set the kid up in a separate business somewhat alike, and say, 'Here, go and run that for a while. If you can't run it, don't come back to me and mess up my business'. What is important is giving the person learning the business increasing responsibility for increasing assets on an increasingly profitable basis. This has to be visible to as many people as you can see. Secrecy, in this case, is gone by the board.

An important role of the board can be to assure the incumbent leader that the person designated as the next leader does now have the skills to run the business. As a result he or she can relax enough to make an exit from the business without worrying that it will collapse:

**Leon Danco**: In the United States, this situation [*the need to decide the date of retirement of the present leader*] is where your board of directors should sit down and say, 'Well, it's time to get out'. It's so often the case that I as a consultant can see this and the board can see it, but the leader himself can't bring himself to leave the business. I sometimes need to remind them to do it. I say to the board: 'I am watching him getting tired. You will have to get him out of this because he is not going to listen to his wife'. But in the United States, this is the board's job and they do it well. I mean, it has to be somebody other than the immediate family telling dad to get out. It has to be somebody he respects.

Despite these many benefits of having a board and thereby formalizing the operations of the family firm, several incumbent CEOs pointed to the tension between the informality of decision-making achieved through having 'family only' on the board and the more formal approach of representing outsiders' views. This opinion was typical of many of our informants:

We've had one director retire, a new one appointed. We've put him in the role of chairman, because we think that a non-executive chairman is required. We haven't yet gone to the point of paying money to a lot of other people from outside to help us manage the organization. And I'm not convinced that we should. I should be. All the literature tells you that you should have a board made up of at least three outside non-executive directors, one of them being the chairman, perhaps only one executive, the managing director. But I'm not so sure, and we see plenty of examples where that type of board doesn't work. For me the jury is still out.

## Summary and Conclusion

The leader of the family owned business has all the same issues of management control as any leader of any business. Our study of effective family firms' strategic responses to environmental contingencies – a major part of the exercise of leadership – showed that there was no simple path through the issues of managing and meeting the pressures inherent in the firm's internal and external environment. Learning *our* business, we saw, was a matter of learning to value the particular qualities of this business, the family business. Achieving this was often a matter of learning from the values and traditions of the previous generation but this time inside the firm. This learning assumed, following with Davis and Tagiuri (1989) that the older and younger generations were also able to meet their respective life-stage needs. In terms of the stage of the business in its life cycle, this stage of learning also meant varying the traditions to meet the needs of a business that had probably moved to a more developed stage.

Leadership of family firms, as for non-family firms, imposes the more complex learning priority of *perspicacity* since, as our quantitative analysis showed, the leader now needs to address the whole gamut of the firm's internal and external uncertainties in developing appropriate management systems. But additionally, in a family business, perspicacity means the leader has to master the demands of being simultaneously a transactional leader and a transformational leader, both leading and managing. Our interview evidence showed that for leaders of family firms, this is achieved through 'informal formality'. Dealing with this paradox means learning to exercise both transactional and transformational approaches to leadership, both formal and 'clan' informal controls simultaneously.

This reinforces the findings of our quantitative evidence about the complexities of leading family businesses. There is no clear or obvious pathway through the problem of learning to lead. Rather than a simple choice, leadership turns out to be a careful balance between apparently opposed approaches. As the firm professionalizes, leaders of family firms typically introduce outsiders, formal boards, complex information gathering systems and other control devices that bring greater formality to the decision making and other leadership practices of the firm. However leaders are likely to do this 'by stealth', that is, in ways that do not interfere with both the perception and the reality that the clan-based, informal approaches are equally valued. And, while acknowledging the need to professionalize the firm, they or others in the firm sometimes still have a yearning for the simpler times of the past.

We will have more to say in Chapter 7 about some patterns of successful control and leadership that emerged from our quantitatively focussed research into successful family businesses. At that point we will see how they relate to the business life cycle. Discerning and implementing successful patterns in the development of control systems in relation to the family firm's external and internal contextual factors is a major learning task of leadership. But before we can come to that, there is at least one other major leadership learning task left, which has its own learning priority and paradox. Some would say it is among the prime tasks of leading the family business: learning to *let go* the family business. It forms the subject of the next chapter.

## References

Bass, B. M. (1990), *Bass and Stogdill's Handbook of Leadership: Theory, Research and Managerial Applications*, 3$^{rd}$ ed., New York, Free Press.

Bass, B. M. and Avolio, B. J. (1990), 'The implications of transactional and transformational leadership for individual, team, and organizational development', *Research in Organizational Change and Development*, vol. 4, pp. 231-72.

Bryman, A. (1999), 'Leadership in Organizations', in S. R. Clegg, C. Hardy and W. R. Nord, *Managing Organizations: Current Issues*, London, Sage.

Bryman, A., Gillingwater, D. and McGuinness, I. (1996), 'Leadership and organizational transformation', *International Journal of Public Administration*, vol. 19, pp. 849-72.

Chung, K., Lubatkin, M., Rogers, R. and Owers, J. (1987), 'Do insiders make better CEO's than outsiders?', *Academy of Management Executive*, vol. 1, no. 3, pp. 325-31.

Dalton, D. and Kesner, I. (1983), 'Inside/Outside Succession and Organizational Size: The Pragmatics of Executive Replacement', *Academy of Management Journal*, vol. 26, no. 4, pp. 736-42.

Dalton, D. and Kesner, I. (1985), 'Organizational performance as an antecedent of Inside/Outside Chief Executive Succession: An empirical assessment', *Academy of Management Journal*, vol. 28, no. 4, pp. 749-62.

Datta, D. and Guthrie, J. (1994), 'Executive Succession: Organizational antecedents of CEO characteristics', *Strategic Management Journal*, vol. 15, pp. 569-77.

Davis, John A. and Tagiuri, R. (1989), 'The Influence of Life Stage on Father-Son Work Relationships in Family Companies', *Family Business Review*, vol. 2, no. 1, Spring, pp. 47-74.

Dyer, Jr., W. G. (1986), *Cultural Change in Family Firms: Anticipating and Managing Business and Family Transitions*, San Francisco, Jossey-Bass.

Foster, Alicia Turner (1995), 'Developing Leadership in the Successor Generation', *Family Business Review*, vol. 8, no. 3, Fall, pp. 201-09.

Lubatkin, M., Chung, K., Rogers, R. and Owers, J. (1989), 'Stockholder reactions to CEO changes in large corporations', *Academy of Management Journal*, vol. 32, pp. 47-68.

Miller, D. (1993), 'Some organizational consequences of CEO succession', *Academy of Management Journal*, vol. 36, no. 3, June, pp. 644-59.

Miner, J. B. (1982), 'The uncertain future of the leadership concept: revisions and clarifications', *Journal of Applied Behavioral Science*, vol. 18, pp. 293-307.

Morrill, C. and Waterhouse, J. (1994), *Chief Executive Officer Turnover, Firm Performance and Accounting Earnings*, AAA Conference, New York.

Robbins, S. P. (2000), *Organizational Behavior*, 9th ed., New Jersey, Prentice-Hall Inc.

Salancik, G. and Pfeffer, J. (1980), 'Effects of Ownership and Performance on Executive Tenure in US Corporations', *Academy of Management Journal*, vol. 23, no. 4, pp. 653-64.

Sant, R. (1988), *Managerial Replacement: Firm Performance and Shareholder Wealth*, Working Paper, University of Iowa.

Schulze, William S., Lubatkin, Michael H., Dino, Richard N. and Buchholtz, Ann K. (2001), 'Agency Relationships in Family Firms: Theory and Evidence', *Organizational Science*, vol. 12, no. 2, March-April, pp. 99-116.

Schwartz, Marc A. and Barnes, Louis B. (1991), 'Outside Boards and Family Businesses: Another Look', *Family Business Review*, vol. 4, no. 3, Fall, pp. 269-85.

Sorensen, R. L. (2000), 'The Contribution of Leadership Style and Practices to Family and Business Success', *Family Business Review*, vol. 13, no. 3, pp. 183-200.

# Chapter 6

# Learning to *Let Go* Our Business

All organizations undergo transitions as they change and this is often most noticeable when a new CEO has been appointed. As a result, considerable attention has been devoted to the issue of CEO succession in firms in general. It has typically has been examined in the context of publicly owned companies, but privately held family businesses also face succession issues, to an extent which means that succession dominates the family research literature (Dyer and Handler, 1994; Wortmann, 1994). In fact, some say that the three most important issues confronting a family business are succession, succession, ... and succession.

In our preceding chapters, we have been examining the stages of learning to manage family businesses in terms of an idea derived from Handy (1994), namely that if we are to cope with the turbulence of life today, we must start by finding ways to organize it in our minds. Framing the confusion is the first step to doing something about it. Part of framing the variety of experiences in learning to run family businesses has been to see them as a series of priorities. These priorities, because of the combination of family and business interests, and because of the need to accommodate both of these with the firm's changing position on the organizational life cycle curve, give rise to complex issues. These are paradoxes, rather than problems in the usual sense. Paradoxes can only be managed, they can't be made to disappear. For the CEOs we talked to who were dealing with issues of succession, or learning to *let go* their business, the need to frame their experiences was even more apparent – and urgent.

## Learning Priority – Prescience

Just as in our earlier chapters which delineated the stages of learning business, learning our business, and learning to lead our business, there is an overriding priority in learning this aspect of leading the firm: the need for prescience to know when and how to let go. So far, everything in the preceding chapters has been directed towards seeing the learner eventually at the helm of the business, gradually becoming an integral part of it. Succession, or passing on the leadership of the business, is also a problem of leadership. But letting go is a paradoxical kind of leadership problem, because it has to do with planning what needs to happen *when the incumbent CEO is no longer there*. That is, the CEO indeed leading, but in order to let go. A further feature of letting go our business is that, contrary to what the words themselves might suggest, letting go is not so much an event as a *process* of transition. Let us now examine the stages of *letting go* the business, and the factors that influence how incumbent CEOs of family business learn to handle this process.

**Succession Issues and the Factors that Influence Succession Decisions**

Our informants, along with Leon Danco, identified two major questions they saw as crucial in managing the process of succession or letting go the family business:

- What needs to happen if the business is going to continue in the family?
- How should the successor be appointed and the retirement process of the present CEO be managed?

Broader matters such as the firm's culture and its stage of development in the business life cycle impinge on these issues. Further, the influence and desires of the family and the motivations of the incumbent CEO regarding his or her future have an impact. Let us examine how these matters influence the two major questions.

**Question 1: What Needs to Happen if the Business is Going to Continue in the Family?**

In this first stage of thinking about 'what comes after', the incumbent CEO confronts the question of whether the business should be sold and to whom. Our sample of informants, as noted earlier, are all second-generation (or later) members of the same family, so the question of family ownership has already been answered at least one time in the affirmative. However, even if the decision is to leave the business in the family, the question arises of what qualities the new leader will need. This is linked to the personal development stages of both the current CEO and the likely heir, as Tagiuri and Davis (1989) have pointed out. Other researchers (see for example, Chrisman, Chua and Sharma, 1998) have given attention to the necessary attributes of successors to family businesses. They found, anticipating our findings on 'valuing values' outlined in Chapter 4, that qualities of 'integrity' and 'commitment to the business' along with 'competence' and a good relationship with the current CEO.

As with so much of what we have seen before, the kind of role the new CEO will take on depends on the life cycle stage the business has reached. The most successful results will come from matching the new leader's role to the stage the business has reached in its life cycle. In Chapter 2 we examined the stages of the business life cycle, and how each stage presents varying managerial role demands on the CEO. Let us recap these stages briefly, this time with a view to understanding the priorities they impose on the leader as he attempts to understand what implications his or her leaving the firm will have for its development.

## The Business Life Cycle

Broadly speaking, before their maturity firms will show 'ascending' characteristics, and after it there is a risk that they will show descending characteristics. Ascending firms are dominated by 'E' or Entrepreneurialism. This manifests itself in a 'permissive' control ethos in which everything is permitted unless it is expressly forbidden. Function dominates form in matters of organizational structure. Political power rests with marketing and sales. The leader of a firm at this stage needs to facilitate convergent thinking, and mobilize the firm's internal change agents. In descending firms, 'A' or Administrative features dominate. The 'A' role may become so disproportionate as to encompass rules about trivia that people respect but no longer understand: 'Administrivism' rules. A bureaucratic control ethos means that everything is forbidden unless expressly permitted, form dominates function in the firm's structure, and political power rests with its finance and accounting functions. The task of the leader is to facilitate divergent thinking, and to mobilize external agents of change.

## Managerial Roles for the Life Cycle Stages

Another way to consider the life cycle stages of the business is to consider the managerial roles they require. At the initiation stage of the business, the role of the CEO is typically that of originator and/or inventor of the idea that will sustain the business. Through the early stages of a firm's development, the leader needs to plan and organize the functions of the firm and later, to guide the implementation of more sophisticated management systems as the firm develops and approaches maturity. At maturity, the firm needs a leader with a grasp of the administrative requirements of this more complex stage of the firm's operation.

However, to avoid the firm moving into a decline stage, the leader – or often, the successor – will need to *re*-organize the firm, and develop a new view of its future. The person needed for this stage may very well not be the founder. The reason for this is that the skills needed to establish a family business and negotiate it successfully through birth and growth stages are not the same as the skills needed to consolidate it into maturity and avoid it moving into a decline. Given the different managerial roles required at different stages of the business life cycle, the current leader might not be the most appropriate person even to select the next leader.

For the purposes of this chapter which is about the special leadership problem of leaving our business, we report results from our interview research with members of family firms where it had been decided to keep the business in the family. Even so, the transfer of power that accompanies the choice of the next person to carry out the CEO role often meant dealing with insecurity, friction and rivalry. We found this could occur both between the incumbent leader and other family members, and among the family members themselves. To avoid these problems some of our CEOs stressed that succession should never entail simply giving the business away, even to a family member who was well trained for the task of leadership. As one CEO in our study put it:

> It's not a succession in the sense that I've *given* this to P. [*her son*]. The family own no shares. I own it all. It is not an automatic thing. P. has bought the trading company. I've got other children besides him, and I think that succession can be quite disastrous.

Clearly, according to this informant, succession should not take place via a non-market-based transfer of wealth. She had several reasons for believing this. First, she felt that transactions carried out on a non-commercial basis would be likely to harm the business. Second, she felt her future security would be adversely affected:

> But if I wasn't prepared to contend with three children who decided that they didn't want P. to have it, or they didn't want me to sell the trading company. I was the one who had done the work in this business, not them. I had decided that at the time I wanted to get out of it, that I would get out of it with some

reward for me. So the property is still mine, not theirs. When I die, there will be plenty left, but I'm not going to have haggling family, as I've seen so often, saying, 'You can't have this, or you can't have that'. What right have they to say that? I haven't won it by succession. It was something that B. [*her husband*] and I started together.

Non-market-based transactions fail to do justice to the hard work of the parent, often the founder of the business. They tend to make successors underestimate the value of what they had received. Third, they tend to create conflict among members of the younger generation who are likely to feel that one or more of them had been disadvantaged. This would be particularly likely if there were several members of the younger generation who expected to inherit.

## Question 2: How Should the Successor be Appointed and the Retirement Process of the Present CEO be Managed?

When appointing a successor, all the issues we have dealt with in our preceding chapters come into view: the selection, training and formal designation of the person who will take over the business. Answering question 2 signals the need for a successor who has learned business, has learned our business (the *family* business) and is ready, now, to learn to *lead* that business in the position of CEO. For now we will assume that, at the time the incumbent CEO announces he or she plans to retire, these stages are well understood, and that someone with the appropriate talent has been selected and has learned the necessary skills.

Whatever means are used to choose the successor, it is important to recognize that the process of succession is just beginning. Careful handling of the changeover to a new CEO and dealing with the present CEO's actual retirement are vital to a successful succession. The need for the present CEO to accept that someone else must eventually take control and to plan for his or her retirement are of paramount importance. Nonetheless, the process is not always an easy one, especially when it comes to setting a definite timetable for the succession process. As one of our interviewees said:

> The experts say that you should set a date and a time, and I disagree with that. I really do. I think that if you say that you would really go into a wind-down mode, and that would have a detrimental effect on a business. I think it's just something that needs to evolve. I think my generation can definitely stay

around too long, but I also think that having put my whole life into it, to some extent it should be my prerogative. I think I'm sensible enough to know when it is time, having begun to work on it, already.

According to Leon Danco, however, this view is fraught with peril. Many family business owners in fact have a great deal of difficulty in recognizing what is the right time to leave. As a result, they have trouble making and sticking to a defined timeframe for leaving the business:

**Interviewer**: In terms of learning for this particular transition we've talked thus far really about the individual learning to depart. What about the needs of the business requiring the departure? Are there ways in which that in itself creates a transition and how can the incumbent be encouraged to think in terms of exit?

**Leon Danco**: […] To put it simply, you have to give him an office on the top floor with no elevator. Compare it to this situation. You have a fine, old talented bookkeeper. She's been with you for a long time, does great work. But you try to sell her on having a computer in the business, she will fight that computer with her dying breath because it will go and obsolete [*sic*] her ability to run the controls. And you have to meet my standard female bookkeeper that keeps the books in the family business, my little old lady with the moustache, she will absolutely will shoot the computer salesman. 'They are useless,' she will say. 'You spend a lot of time doing nothing. I can do it just with my own two hands.' And the business owner is like the little old lady with the computer. He will not allow something to sneak in there – especially the next leader – that makes its absolute dominance felt over the structure he has created.

[…]

You can't encourage him to leave by making him feel he has got to jump ship. I have not seen anyone leave where it was done like that. The leader has got to do it to himself, allow it to be done by himself. And he has got to feel reasonably comfortable. You have to get his exit statement planned out. You have to have his management team in top condition. You have to have all of his children, his nephews and nieces, the young generation all happily singing the chorus together and no fights. And that often doesn't happen. It becomes a case of the leader saying 'give me utopia' and then I will step down gracefully. And of course, it's hard to find utopia, so it won't happen.

## The CEO as Hero

Our CEO and Leon Danco, despite the apparent differences in their viewpoints, are both aware there are several potential barriers to the CEO's orderly and happy exit from the business. Leading in order *not* to lead is a difficult business. Following Handy's suggestion, it is helpful to try to frame the issue in order to better understand and manage it. One useful way of thinking about the barriers to exit from the business is to consider the role of the CEO as a kind of 'hero' of the business. As Sonnenfeld (1988) and also Sonnenfeld and Spence (1989) point out, to think of the leader in this way is not an exaggeration if we consider anthropological views of the 'hero' phenomenon. According to the archetypal view of heroes outlined in Campbell's (1949) classic anthropological study, there are three distinct life stages that characterize their ascension to heroic status. The first is a time of *separation from society*. In terms of learning the family business, we can recognize this stage in period that the future CEO typically spends away from the business – sometimes without a definite aim of returning to it. This period is the stage of learning business – the first stage in our typology of learning stages. The second is *a period of continual trials*. We can consider the eventual leader's period of learning the business and having to show he or she deserves its leadership as coinciding with this stage. It corresponds to learning *our* business – the second stage in our typology. The third stage is one of *triumphant re-integration*. The recognition the CEO enjoys as he or she assumes the leadership of the business and gains the confidence of other members of the firm corresponds to this stage. This corresponds to 'learning to lead our business' – the third phase in our typology of learning stages. The question arises, however, of how heroes are to deal with the prospect of no longer being the hero, inevitable in letting go of the business.

## Heroic Stature and Heroic Mission

While heroes – or at least good leaders – are vital, the hero of today can become the tyrant of tomorrow. Our informant showed in the previous quote that he is aware of this possibility and wants to avoid it. But, according to Sonnenfeld (1988), and Sonnenfeld and Spence (1989) there are two specific exit barriers that he and other CEOs are likely to stumble against in the process of learning to let go their business: the hero's stature, and the hero's mission. Both are part of the hero's self-concept. According to Sonnenfeld, *heroic stature* refers to the unique position of power that top leaders hold. *Heroic mission* refers to the unique ability to run the business that the leaders often feel they have (Sonnenfeld and Spence, 1989, p. 358). CEOs may be more or less troubled by the prospect of relinquishing their heroic stature and their heroic mission, and these differences allow us to distinguish their approaches to retirement. The following four approaches to retirement, adapted from Sonnenfeld's typology, illustrate both dangerous and more benign possibilities.

- **Monarchs** are the most troubled by both barriers to both barriers to exit from the business. They do not leave until forced, and this may happen only through death or a 'palace revolt' in the form of resignations or ultimatums from senior managers.
- **Generals** long for their lost heroic stature. They leave only when forced, but finally do so willingly. However, they *plan to return*, and may come out of retirement to rescue the firm from the real or imaginary failings of their successors.
- **Governors** are similarly untroubled by exit – at least on the surface, though they long for a new mission after retirement. Their approach to leaving is to rule for a bounded period only, making a clean break when the moment for exit comes. They then genuinely carry out the clean exit strategy and maintain little contact with the business thereafter.
- **Ambassadors** are the least troubled by either barrier to exit. They leave willingly and maintain contact with the business in an advisory capacity during the transition process. Their exits are graceful.

Figure 6.1 illustrates the possibilities.

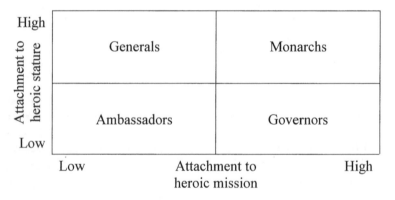

**Figure 6.1     Retirement options for CEOs**

In summary, monarchs and generals have least mastery over heroic stature and most frustration with the process of exit from family firms. Monarchs and generals are prevalent in family firms and have contributed to the wealth of research literature on the peculiar difficulties which surround the succession issue in family business. Ambassadors and governors, by contrast, deal with the loss of heroic stature much better, and seem relatively untroubled by frustration over the impending loss of their heroic mission (Sonnenfeld and Spence, 1989, p. 359).

## Pathways Through the Paradox of Leading to Let Go

Now that we are aware of the nature of the barriers to exit, it is time to consider how best to overcome them. The keys to this, according to both Leon Danco and our informants, lie with the timing and general management of the succession process. The recommended pathways involve a number of parties: the incumbent CEO, the other members of the family, the 'outside' managers, members of the board, and any non-family owners. In summary, the pathways our informants typically pointed to suggested the process falls into three phases:

- developing a defined timeline for retirement;
- creating management development systems;
- sticking to the plan.

Let us look at each of these in turn.

*Pathway 1: Develop a Defined Timeline for Retirement*

In contrast to the views of the CEO quoted at the beginning of this chapter, it was generally accepted among CEOs in our sample that it is better to have a timetable for the retirement process. Moreover, the timetable tends to work better if the current CEO has been the person to develop it. This is particularly true of the current CEO is also the founder of the business. The consequences of failing to develop a timetable are often that the issues of heroic stature and heroic mission are never properly considered. According to Leon Danco and our respondents, or most of them, developing a defined timeline for leaving our business usually meant starting to do this early. There needs to be a set of defined succession plans for senior managers as well, including those who are never likely to be appointed to the top job. A major obstacle to this is the CEO's sense of heroic mission, or the belief that that he or she alone was capable of running the business. One of our informants now regretted not having done more to encourage others in the idea that they too could deal with the CEO's 'heroic mission':

> **Informant**: I suppose that it's my own fault. As they [*other family members*] came on into the business, I should have taught them and given them a more managerial role in certain things. We usually still do discuss things, but [...] I just kept doing it, and you think you're never going to die, never going to get sick and all this stupid sort of thing. It's silly, but it's happened in so many places.

A further obstacle, according to Leon Danco, is that confronting the sense of loss that comes from thinking about life following the eventual and inevitable exit from the business. This, together with concern about the capabilities of the successor, is often the most difficult task the leader faces in the succession process. As Leon Danco says:

> **Leon Danco**: [...] for many business owners, the retirement process seems like a cross between euthanasia and castration. It's something the average business owner is never going to look at willingly.

As a result, the only solution is to get the incumbent CEO to recognize the necessity of adopting a definite timetable for departure. In this respect, the incumbent needs to be persuaded to look at the task of running the business as having a defined finishing time, just like any other job in the professional world:

> **Leon Danco**: [...] the first thing I ask business owners who want to get in touch with me, to come to my seminars, to consult with me, is, 'Do you plan on leaving this business alive or you just want do it until you drop dead and let the pieces fall after you are gone?'. 'Will you retire before the end of your natural life span?'. They [*family business owners*] always say to me, 'Oh, I know when I am going to retire – when I can't do it'. And I say, 'No, I want a fixed date. No other business in the professional world works like that. Everybody in the professional world realizes that they are going to get kicked out eventually. You don't hang on until you choose to leave'.

[...]

And I tell him [*the incumbent CEO*] to look at it this way. If a university told your child walking in that it would graduate him when he was smarter than his teachers, the kid would never get out. According to that logic there would be just no way the son would ever get to run the family firm. But I remind him [*the incumbent CEO*] that when someone enters university there's a deal. Some forty months after the student enters the university, it is going to graduate him – maybe with honours – from the university because he fulfils what he is supposed to do within a given length of time to the standard expected of him. And so dad, you too are going to retire under certain conditions.

It needs to be done early because to delay the decision about the leader's retirement and how the firm is to continue is to run the risk of incurring major financial penalties. As Leon Danco puts it:

**Leon Danco**: Deciding about how and when to leave is an emotional hurdle of some height and it has to be crossed early on in the process because if the business is not to be turned over to the children you need to say to yourself, 'Let's plan on selling, let's build up the assets, get maximum value'.

## *Pathway 2: Create Management Development Systems*

How CEOs of family businesses learn to value and create management development systems has been the subject of our three immediately preceding chapters where we considered what learning stages are involved for those who aspire to run a family business. We considered the need for the learner first to go outside the business, then to learn to appreciate the business's philosophies and especially the value to be derived from being a family business, the role of the board in providing an objective set of reviewers of the learner's progress, and so on. Finally, the learner manages the complexities of the firm's strategic approaches to its environment. Through all these management development stages, however, we were looking at them from the point of view of the eventual, aspiring owner, not from the point of view of the person who would need to relinquish the business. According to Leon Danco, creating management development systems for an eventual successor, even though that person is a son or daughter, is only possible if the CEO confronts the discomfort of learning to let go: .

**Leon Danco**: [...] If you want this business to continue, if you think that 'my business might continue', if you stick that phrase up on the wall and don't lie to yourself about it, then that's achievable, we can get that done. [...] But there's a price to pay and that is that 'you will retire'. Because until you retire there is no commencement for the child's activities as the leader of the firm.

Some of our informants who felt succession had been managed well in their family businesses – and who felt they were managing it well themselves – agreed that it was important to 'have a clear line of succession', that is, to know 'who would be the next boss'. The following view was typical of this group:

> As I said before succession has to be planned if the family business is to survive. I would say that is the single most important thing in a family business. There has to be *one* family member in charge. No matter how equal everyone is, there still has to be one in charge. And it's important to know well in advance who that person will be.

In this scenario overt planning had been important. In other family businesses, however, where people were just as convinced that the succession process was working well, a tacit approach was felt to be just as effective. When these CEOs looked back, it seemed that succession arrangements had arisen more or less naturally and as a matter of tacit understanding, rather than through formal planning and management development of someone previously designated as the anointed successor:

> **Interviewer**: How did your father indicate to your brothers that it was going to be you?
>
> **Informant**: Well I was just doing the job, and it wasn't hard to see. I was giving the orders.

Who will be the next boss is not the only issue that needs to be dealt with early, whether openly or tacitly. It is also important for the CEO to consider how he or she will cope with the fears of retirement, and also for the family to be sensitive to his or her needs. The CEO's spouse – generally assumed by our informants to be the wife – has a critical role to play here. As Katie and Leon Danco put it:

> **Katie Danco**: The father has to have something to retire *to*, not *from*. If he has something to retire to, then you are going to get him turn over the reins. If he has nothing in his life except his business, you are never going to get him out.
>
> **Leon Danco**: This is where the wonderful supportive spouse, in most of my experience, the spouse wife, is so essential. Because if you take the spouse away by divorce, by death, or something and dad is all alone, it means the chances of getting him to stay out of that business are very remote. In my practice, I see no chance, in fact. But when we have a spouse, we go home. If I

have Katie to go home to, we can have another life. The CEO, like me, can afford to say to someone else, 'I can let you run the show. I have done it for all these years. I expect you to be well regarded by your peers and my peers. I will turn over this place to you. I am going home with Katie'.

Our informants were also strongly in agreement about the need to have an activity to retire to, not merely a business to retire from. For many, this was tied up with the issue of remaining involved with the business, but at a distance, say by becoming non-executive directors on the board, or simply having a physical presence around the business.

## *Pathway 3: Stick to the Plan*

Our informants – with a few exceptions – felt that they would be able to work out a specific retirement plan, and stick to it when the time came. Nevertheless, they pointed to many instances when they felt the retirement plans of CEOs they knew had not been developed or carried out well. One reason, in their opinion, that incumbent CEOs sometimes fail to manage succession issues well, including training a suitable replacement CEO and then sticking to their timeframe to leave the business, is that they don't know where they can learn about such matters and achieve the level of confidence that will enable them to stick to the plan. Building a network of peers who can empathize and share the departing CEO's hopes and fears for the future is an important part of coping with the process and therefore being able to stick to the retirement plan. As Leon Danco put it:

> **Leon Danco**: Retirement is a touchy issue and it takes a loving wife and kids that are considerate. I say to the children, 'Be kind to your fathers as they get close to retirement. They have no experience in being kept as a pet. In fact it's against everything he knows to be kept as a pet. You know, everybody wants to be somebody'.

Many of our informants pointed out that Australia's Family Business Association and other similar networks can help here. It is linked to the world-wide family business 'movement' via the Family Business Network (FBN) in Europe and the Family Firms Institute (FFI) in the United States which can provide similar advice.

The establishment of a board of directors can also be helpful now, if this hasn't been done already. This is because developing and sticking to a specific retirement plan also involves seeking consensus. While the CEO needs to develop a plan that he or she feels comfortable with, if the plan is developed by the incumbent CEO *alone* without consulting other members of the family and the business, it is unlikely to succeed. It is important to create a shared vision of the future. This can be also done through formal family councils. These gatherings, held annually or more frequently, can also help make the extended family aware of the possibilities of establishing a career in the family firm, and what recruitment standards apply.

We have touched on this issue in Chapter 3, when we noticed how often leaders of family businesses said that they reserved the right to look outside for new talent to enter the family firm. In the context of the retirement process of the family business leader, the same gatherings can become a venue for members of the family to discuss their values and expectations of the business and for one another as they enter a new phase. According to Leon Danco, the board will probably also have a major role in this stage. It is as much an emotional support role as a technical one:

> **Leon Danco**: When it comes to the leader's retirement [...] all outside advisors do is to make the obvious, obvious. And do what you want to do, this will always be the problem. The leader will be lonely. He will be scared, tired, running out of time, misunderstood. He will need other human beings in the process. He's got to get the wisdom to leave from somewhere, whether it comes from the pastor reading the Bible, or from talking to himself in the dark. He will have to have a conversation with somebody. But it's a very personal issue. I think it needs a creation of a group of professionals. You are going to attach this issue to the people you have drawn from the current professional market to advise the business. They are going to need to enlarge the topic of discussion beyond their professional spheres.

## Summary and Conclusion

The three pathways outlined above to manage the process of leaving our business make the succession process appear logical, even if the problem itself is a paradox: 'leading in order to let go'. However according to our informants being a logical process does not make it an easy one. While new leaders can be catalysts for change, factors at the individual and the firm level can make changes messy and difficult, and this is equally true of succession. As a result, sometimes change or succession can be aborted altogether. Equally, the continuing presence of 'retired' CEOs who have not accepted their new status and found a new role will extend the succession process indefinitely and make it still more difficult. CEOs have to deal with the fact that while they had become accustomed to seeing themselves as the leader, they have to become willing outcasts. That is, they must welcome the presence of being displaced by their own anointed heir.

Yet heirs who are active and already capably involved in the business, perhaps through a long-standing mentoring process, are essential to the continuation of the business. Well before they move into the top position, they need to be perceived as good performers whom others can trust to lead the business in future. Equally important is that the designated new CEO be seen to be serious about new strategies or management practices he or she plans to introduce and to have the expertise to introduce them. Making sure all this happens in a timely and orderly way is in large measure the task of the incumbent CEO. It means he or she needs to plan for his or her position as the 'anointed one' to become that of the outcast.

As a result, learning to let go the family business is yet another aspect of the paradoxical qualities of leading, since it requires the leader to plan for when he or she will no longer be leading. In essence, the task of learning to leave consists in leading *in order to let go*. The paradox is that where learning the family business in the earlier stages has involved learning, achieving, justifying one's place as the anointed successor, this stage of learning involves the reverse – the anointed leader must place himself or herself in what feels like the position of a voluntary outcast. To add to the difficulty, most of our informants agree it needs to be done early – sometimes not much later than the time the CEO takes over the reins of power. It involves a mental dissociation from the firm that is conscious and deliberate often just when the firm typically needs the most direct and detailed involvement by those running it – typically as it reaches maturity.

The pathways through the paradox of leading to let go, effectively moving from the position of leader to willing outcast, while difficult, nevertheless have some clarity to them. They include planning early for the CEO's retirement, creating management development plans, and making and keeping to a clear plan for the whole process. They also include adopting a future role in the business that, preferably, resembles an 'ambassador' or 'governor' relationship with the firm.

Learning to deal with succession – letting go the family business – shares an important characteristic with the other phases of learning we have discussed. The problem of leaving the business, like the other paradoxes, cannot be made to disappear. Yet, despite the pattern of increasing management complexity the problem of family business leadership presents, there are some recurring patterns in the ways successful Australian family businesses have tackled leadership tasks. In line with our earlier discoveries, the stage the firm has reached in its business life cycle provides some important insights into these approaches. So it is time now to summarize some of the approaches that work – to sketch the profiles of successful Australian family businesses whose leaders have demonstrably managed the intrinsic paradoxes of linking family and business.

## References

Campbell, Joseph (1949), *The Hero with a Thousand Faces*, Princeton, New Jersey, Princeton University Press.

Chrisman, James J., Chua, Jess H. and Sharma, Pramodita (1998), 'Important Attributes of Successors in Family Businesses: An Exploratory Study', in *Family Business Review*, vol. 11, no. 1, March, pp. 19-34.

Davis, John A. and Tagiuri, R. (1989), 'The Influence of Life Stage on Father-Son Work Relationships in Family Companies', *Family Business Review*, vol. 2, no. 1, Spring, pp. 47-74.

Dyer, W. G., Jr., and Handler, W. (1994), 'Entrepreneurship and family business: Exploring the connections', *Entrepreneurship Theory and Practice*, vol. 19, pp. 71-83.

Handy, Charles (1994), *The Empty Raincoat*, London, Random House.

Sonnenfeld, J. (1988), *The Hero's Farewell: What Happens When CEOs Retire*, Oxford, Oxford University Press.

Sonnenfeld, J. and Spence, P. (1989), 'The Parting Patriarch of a Family Firm', *Family Business Review*, vol. 2, no. 4, Winter, pp. 355-75.

Wortmann, M. S., Jr. (1994), 'Theoretical foundations for family-owned businesses: A conceptual and research based paradigm', *Family Business Review*, vol. 7, no. 1, pp. 3-27.

# Chapter 7

# Profiles and Patterns that Work

So far, we have examined how owners of family businesses have managed the various stages involved in learning business, learning *our* business, learning to *lead* our business and learning to *let go* our business. These emerged from considering the evidence from interviews with incumbent CEOs as well as quantitative evidence about how family firms have been successfully managed through a series of transitions to become medium-sized and in some cases large businesses. We examined the priorities for each learning stage and the paradoxes these create. We also reported on pathways through the paradoxes as they appeared through the eyes of the CEOs.

In Chapters 3 and 4, 'Learning Business' and 'Learning *Our* Business', we noted that the influence of the organizational life cycle became more prominent as earlier stages of learning gave way to subsequent stages. As the aspiring CEO learnt business in general, the pathway through the associated learning paradox involved going outside the business. At this stage, the pathway was virtually universal, although the business life cycle stage could suggest some strategic choices about where the outside learning might be carried out.

After the learner returns to the family firm to learn *our* business, however, the stage the firm has reached in its life cycle has more salience for the tasks of learner. It suggests, sometimes strongly and painfully, the ways the learner needs both to appreciate the special qualities and philosophies of the family business, and yet often to reject the detail of how they have manifested themselves in the past. In short, the learner 'continues' these philosophies and qualities, but continues them 'differently' because of changes in the firm's position in its life cycle.

In Chapter 5, 'Learning to Lead our Business', we examined the complexity of the context factors that the family business leader needs to understand and manage. We also saw how the approach to family business became a matter of managing 'formal informality', that is, the valuing of the family nature of the business through the use of clan controls at the same time as formalizing its control mechanisms. The implication of the burgeoning complexities of the leadership task was that there was no simple recipe for dealing with the task of leadership.

However this need not mean the situation is totally chaotic and random for CEOs of family businesses. It is useful at this point to return briefly to the correlation results of our quantitative research to consider another way of considering the firm's internal environment – its position on the business life cycle stage – and how this relates to the strategic management choices which form such a major part of the task of leadership. In addition, we will consider interview and other evidence which allows us to build detailed profiles of a proportionate sub-set of family businesses in our sample which have reached specific stages of the business life cycle. These quantitative and qualitative results, especially when they are considered in conjunction with the results reported in Chapter 5 about the strategic choices of leaders of successful family businesses, suggest, if not blueprints, at least some consistent profiles and patterns for success of Australian family businesses.

## Life Cycle Influences on Family Firm Management and Control

As we noted in Chapter 2, firms follow developmental stages. In that chapter, following the discussion of the Adizes model of the firm life cycle, we proposed a summary model based on four stages – (1) *Entrepreneurial*, (2) *Collectivity*, (3) *Formalization and Control*, and (4) *Elaboration of Structure* – which captures the essence of a firm's development. Given our focus on second (and later generations) family firms, our study concentrates on firms in stages 2, 3 and 4 of the business life cycle curve, that is, firms that have survived the entrepreneurial phase of the founder. The theoretical framework we discussed in Chapter 2 allows us to examine in detail how the life cycle stage of family owned businesses correlates with aspects of their systems of management and control. In other words, we examine how strategic patterns in family business CEOs' management choices reflect the firms' stage of development.

To ascertain the stage of life cycle development of firms in our sample we relied upon a proxy based on a set of structural measures suggested in the literature as coinciding with developmental stages. On this basis, 17 per cent of our sample were classified as being in the *Collectivity* stage, 75 per cent of the sample in the *Formalization and Control* stage, and 8 per cent of the sample in the *Elaboration of Structure* stage.

Table 7.1 presents the firms in terms of their position on the life cycle curve, together with the average characteristics of the firms in each stage. Table 7.2 presents the ways the CEOs of these firms experienced aspects of their firms' internal and external environment. Further, quantitative data concerning these internal and external environment characteristics is presented in Table A.13 of the Appendix.

### Table 7.1   Firm demographics

| Average | Stage 2: Collectivity | Stage 3: Formalization and Control | Stage 4: Elaboration of Structure |
|---|---|---|---|
| Number of employees | 74 | 99 | 238 |
| Number of years in business | 46 | 46 | 47 |
| Number of generations | 2.63 | 2.71 | 2.57 |
| % of firms in each stage | 17% | 75% | 8% |

*Source*: Adapted from Moores and Mula (2000), p. 133.

### Table 7.2   Emergent stage profiles

| Characteristics | Stage 2: Collectivity | Stage 3: Formalization and Control | Stage 4: Elaboration of Structure |
|---|---|---|---|
| Levels of environmental uncertainty | Moderate | Moderate | Moderate |
| Level of product differentiation | Medium | Medium | Medium |
| Structure | Centralized | Decentralized | Decentralized |
| Content of control systems | Simple | Sophisticated | More sophisticated |
| Form of control systems | Narrow | Broad | Broader |

*Source*: Adapted from Moores and Mula (2000).

Tables 7.1 and 7.2 as well as Table A.13 in the Appendix, which provides detailed quantitative data, reveal that the pattern of characteristics of family owned businesses across the three stages of development generally reflects increasing levels of sophistication in management systems as firms develop. As we saw in Chapter 5, all firms perceive moderate levels of environmental uncertainty emanating from *Technoeconomic* sources and *Competition and Constraint* factors. However

*Formalization and Control* stage firms perceive these uncertainties to be the highest. This perhaps reflects the fact that these firms tend to have diversified to a slightly greater extent than either *Collectivity* stage or *Elaboration of Structure* stage firms. Because of this diversification these family firms operate in a greater number of markets and have to take account of more areas of development.

The strategies pursued by all firms rely most heavily upon *Product Differentiation* measures and, to a lesser extent, what we have labelled *Marketing* activities. As noted above, *Formalization and Control* firms undertake more diversification than either *Elaboration of Structure* or *Collectivity* firms, but it is by no means a major feature of their underlying strategy. In fact, it could be said that such moves represent distractions from their core business.

At a structural level all firms are relatively centralized. Only modest levels of delegation prevail in even the largest of family firms. Again, *Formalization and Control* firms seem to delegate slightly more of their decisions to lower management levels than do their counterparts in other stages of development. But this may be merely a reflection of the fact that they have diversified into more business lines. The biggest difference, which of course largely defines the stages, occurs with the structuring of activities. The *Elaboration of Structure* firms have by far the highest levels of divisionalization and departmentalization. The *Formalization and Control* firms are moderately divisionalized but the *Collectivity* firms display much lower levels of structure.

The content of the formal control systems in particular reflects increasing sophistication as firms grow and develop. This indicates an increasing reliance upon these formal systems as family firms mature. This is consistent with an increasing level of professionalism in the management of family firms as they increase in size and complexity. However by far the heaviest reliance is upon *Financial Reporting* by all firms irrespective of their stage of development. In the early stages of firm development, *Operational Controls* and advice from *External* sources such as consultants both rank as moderately important forms of control. But as firms grow and develop they tend to develop internal *Management Controls* instead of relying on external consultants. Further more, these management controls tend to be relatively more important than *Operational Controls* as firms grow beyond *Entrepreneurial* and *Collectivity* stages.

Increased importance is placed on the *Timeliness* and the *Scope of Information* as firms develop through these stages. More timely and broadly based information is far more significant in the control of *Elaboration of Structure* firms than for *Collectivity* firms.

## Learning Tasks for Survival and Growth

This quantitative analysis of life cycle characteristics and their correlation with aspects of the family firm's internal and external environment suggests that these elements of the firm's context are closely linked to the level of sophistication of management and controls. The firm's control systems need to be an internally consistent package of strategies, structures and systems congruent with both the demands of the external environment and the stage of development of the family firm. In this way, control systems must dynamically evolve as businesses grow and mature. As a result, we can derive a first 'learning task' that seems crucial for the success of Australian family businesses:

- Learning task 1: Managers of family firms should adopt management systems which are adequate for the demands of their external and internal environments, as well as their firm's stage of development.

This guideline is a complex one, since there are three issues which test the adequacy of management systems: the external environment, the internal environment and the stage of the firm's development.

### The External Environment

Our study, as reported in Chapter 5, examined correlations of management systems with two different sources of uncertainty in the external environment. The first was uncertainty arising from the technoeconomic environment, that is, scientific/technological change as well as the economic change associated with output markets in which many new products are marketed. The second source of environmental uncertainty was competition and constraints. This includes both the intensity of competition for raw materials and human resource inputs and the market realities of price competition and external regulatory constraints.

Contrary to what we might have expected from some overseas studies (see, for example, Gordon and Narayanan, 1984), environmental uncertainties appear only moderately associated with control system characteristics. Specifically:

- When high uncertainty arises from a changing technoeconomic environment, family firms tend to increase the computerization of their accounting systems to provide information in a timely fashion.
- When high uncertainty arises from external constraints and competition, family owned businesses rely more heavily on conventional reports. There was a consensus among our respondents that the level of external constraints was increasing. Despite this, family firms have yet to identify appropriate ways of controlling these externally induced uncertainties.

## The Internal Environment

Let us now consider this learning task in relation to the internal environment, namely firm strategies and structures.

*The internal environment and firm strategies*  Compared with the elements of the external environment, we saw that firm strategies were more strongly correlated with the development of more complex management systems. Firm strategies are associated with both the content and the form of control information. Specifically, our study showed that:

- When family firms pursue diversification strategies they develop more sophisticated management controls and, to a lesser extent, financial reports.
- When firms pursue marketing oriented strategies, they develop their operational controls.
- When family firms pursue product differentiation strategies, they value information in the form of broad historical data external to the firm such as economic conditions, population growth and technological developments, together with other non-economic data especially if it relates to possible future events.

*The internal environment and firm structure*  The structure of family firms also affects both the content and the form of controls. Systems changes largely accompany structural changes by being introduced together as a package of internally consistent controls. We found, in particular, that:

- When family owned firms establish departments and divisions, they assign cost and profit centre financial responsibilities to managers. Such financial responsibilities are moderately reinforced by emphasizing managerial performance evaluation and having managers actively participate in preparing budgets.

- When family owned firms divisionalize their structures they also develop their operational controls and financial reports.
- When family owned firms delegate authority to lower level managers within divisional structures, they develop more sophisticated forms of both management controls and computerized accounting systems.

## Life Cycle Stage

The *average* profiles set out in Table 7.2 show that family firms, irrespective of their stage of development, typically experience medium levels of uncertainty. Their strategies for dealing with this involve formulating and implementing moderate level of product differentiation. However the internal arrangements for reinforcing these measures vary across stages as the structures and systems become progressively more sophisticated in each stage. Specifically, while *Collectivity* firms use centralized management supported by simple and narrow management information systems, later stage firms adopt increasingly decentralized management structures with sophisticated and broadly based systems. The greatest levels of sophistication are evident in Stage 4 firms. Table 7.3 summarizes these results again in terms of the salience of clan, bureaucratic and market-based controls for firms at different stages of the business life cycle.

**Table 7.3    Salience of control types at different life cycle stages**

| Control type | Stage 2: Collectivity | Stage 3: Formalization and Control | Stage 4: Elaboration of Structure |
| --- | --- | --- | --- |
| Clan | **Most salient** | Less salient | Least salient |
| Bureaucratic | Least salient | **Most salient** | Less salient |
| Market-based | Least salient | More salient | **Most salient** |

*Source*: Adapted from Moores and Mula (2000), p. 96.

We saw some departures from these patterns in our cases but not all departures were equally effective. In some cases, a lack of adequate formal management or inconsistent management did not detract from the overall effectiveness of family firms. In these cases there was a strong sense of corporate mission and direction, and it seems likely that the 'shortcomings' of formal management were compensated by the presence of strong clan controls. The shared beliefs and values of family members and managers ensured that the firm continued to prosper. On the other hand, there were difficulties in firms where there were inadequate formal management systems and *also* internal 'family' problems and disagreements.

We found no firm where formal management systems were adequate, but where the family was in disagreement. So it is difficult to tell whether it is the formal management system or the informal family system that dominates in the effective control of family firms across their stages of development. Perhaps we can say that the development of formal management systems goes some way towards overcoming family disagreements by clarifying the business issues for family consideration. The patterns revealed in individual cases are presented and discussed in the following sections.

## Learning Tasks Derived from Firm Profiles

Four further Learning Tasks crucial for firm survival and growth emerged from the stage of the study in which interview evidence from the CEOs was combined with information which allowed us to assess the stage of their firm's development. They are:

- Learning Task 2: Management approaches should form an *internally consistent* package of strategies, structures and systems.
- Learning Task 3: Management systems must dynamically evolve as the business grows and matures.
- Learning Task 4: Professionalism in management is vital for systems development.
- Learning Task 5: Without succession plans, professionalization of the firm is seriously inhibited.

To see how these learning tasks emerge, let us examine the individual case firm analyses. We assessed 11 case firms: two in the second stage of development, eight in the third stage of development, and one in the fourth stage of development, comparing each with the average profile of firms in its stage of development. The number of firms assessed in each stage reflect the proportions of firms in these stages in the sample. The characteristics of each firm are summarized in Table 7.4 below. (The real identity of the firms has been masked by the use of fictitious firm names.)

**Table 7.4    Case firm characteristics**

| Firm Label | Industry | Turnover | Employees | Stage* |
|---|---|---|---|---|
| P B Hardware | Hardware retail | $3-5m | 35 | 2 |
| Display Services | Display cabinets | $3-5m | 42 | 2 |
| B F Constructions | Building | $10-20m | 26 | 3 |
| M W Metals | Metal fabrication | $1-3m | 29 | 3 |
| H M Hire | Hire services | $3-5m | 70 | 3 |
| A B Carr | Motor dealership | $50-100m | 150 | 3 |
| R X Engineering | Project management | $5-10m | 170 | 3 |
| C K Meats | Meat processing | $50-100m | 290 | 3 |
| K F Foods | Food processing | $50-100m | 300 | 3 |
| L F Transport | Road transport | $100-500m | 4,000 | 3 |
| S F Printers | Printing | $10-20m | 80 | 4 |

* Stage of life cycle development (see Table 7.1).

**Collectivity (Stage 2) Firms**

The average profile for firms at this stage of development reflects an interpersonal management strategy. Managers in *Collectivity* stage family firms rely on simple systems and value relatively narrowly focused information.

The two cases studied in this life cycle stage however, both pursued higher levels of product differentiation than is typical for firms in this early stage of development. While their particular industry settings undoubtedly influenced their strategies, their management assessed their underlying levels of uncertainty as medium. We would have expected that this increased differentiation would have been supported in some way by either formal or informal controls. In particular, if these firms were to use more sophisticated management or at least more broadly based information they could achieve both provide adequate and consistent management.

The approach adopted by *Display Services* management was to place great importance on broadly based information when making decisions.

This goes some way to meeting their control needs but the strength of compensatory clan controls in this case was less reliable. The firm was in the process of an extended transition associated with succession. The second generation CEO was building a new management team in much the same way as his father had done during his tenure. He was still learning to lead the business since the succession had not been as well planned as it could have been. Our view is that there are inadequate controls for the level of differentiation, but that the firm is trying to deal with this by gathering a broad array of information. To sustain this level of differentiation, the firm will need to develop its formal controls if it is to grow.

*P B Hardware* appeared to rely on limited systems to support its extensive differentiation and market oriented strategies in its highly uncertain price competitive market. Its world has changed dramatically from the time the business was founded about seventy ago, yet the systems are still largely those that had been put in place during the term of the entrepreneurial founder. This case clearly reflects the problems that emerge when managerial structures are not established that facilitate ongoing strategic management and succession.

*P B Hardware's* initial management structure was the family structure. This was adequate during the term of the founder as patriarch of the family and head of the business. During the next generation, three sons assumed equal collective responsibility. This might have been appropriate if the firm had wished to remain in the *Collectivity* stage, however, it proved difficult especially as some family members had growth objectives for the business. The clan's values were no longer convergent and the business experienced two break ups, when branches of the family left the core business. The firm continues to rely upon simple systems centred largely around financial accounting reports and still has no explicit managerial structure to take it beyond the *Collectivity* stage. The external environment requires the firm to use differentiation and marketing based strategies to survive, but these must be reinforced by adequate and consistent controls. Such controls have yet to be developed in *P B Hardware* which understandably is struggling to survive. The abiding impression here was that after the leadership of the founder all subsequent 'leadership' was transactional rather than transformational, as no successor was the designated leader responsible for providing a strategic direction. This is an important lesson for family businesses, namely that someone has to assume leadership responsibilities, even if the firm is still at a *Collectivity* stage.

The importance of Guideline 3, *the need for management systems to evolve in a dynamic way as the firms grow and mature*, is already clear from these firms which are still in an early stage of development. We will see more of this pathway, as well as Guideline 4, the need for *professionalism in management to develop systems*, and Guideline 5, the need for *succession plans to professionalize the firm* as we examine firms in the *Formalization and Control* stages and *Elaboration of Structure* stages of the life cycle.

## Formalization and Control (Stage 3) Firms

The majority of firms and cases in our sample were in this middle-level developmental stage. On average they have moved to more decentralized structures with broadly based sophisticated control systems. The transitions to these administrative control strategies are consistent with their increasing size and complexity. In this sense, they are only different from stage 4 firms in terms of the extent to which these formal control measures have been adopted. However the individual firms present a diversity of responses that vary in effectiveness.

### Stage 3 Firms Facing Moderate or Low Uncertainty

Interestingly, only one firm of all those in stage 3, *K F Foods*, exemplifies the average profile with adequate and consistent controls for its context. *K F Foods* is a relatively large, well established business that has benefited from the professionalization that occurred when it was merged with much larger public companies. According to the present chairman, the firm learned much of its current management systems during these associations. The family has now 'retrieved' full management and ownership of the firm and is particularly sophisticated in terms of its use of broadly based information to manage its diverse range of food-related businesses. This highly successful family business stresses business over family, and its early stages of development proactively split the business to avoid too many family demands on what was then a more limited business.

*R X Engineering* possibly represents a case of over-control, especially in the light of its assessment of low external uncertainties. But its origin and history provide some insight. The family dimension in this business is less pronounced than in others because of an acrimonious split some years ago and the subsequent near failure of the firm. The current managing director overcame these difficulties with considerable entrepreneurial initiative in rebuilding a focused business. He installed professional managers to develop sophisticated financial systems. The firm now allows the managing director to devote more time and effort to strategic issues rather than the day-to-day operation and control of the business.

Two other firms at this stage that identify moderate levels of uncertainty have chosen different strategic responses. *B F Constructions* displays very limited differentiation, while *M H Hire* is more in line with the average profile with a mid-level differentiation strategy.

*B F Construction*'s long history has been punctuated by periods of high diversification that have in recent times endangered the survival of the family business. The current management is undertaking a strategic realignment aimed at returning the firm to its core construction business. Notwithstanding its age of 150 years, the firm reflects a stage 3 profile: it has a relatively centralized management structure and associated controls. However, the levels of uncertainty and degree of price competition in the industry suggest that more sophisticated controls will have to be implemented as the firm consolidates its position in this stage of development. In the meantime, relying more on broadly based information would help increase the level of control given the seemingly little convergence in family values relative to business strategies. This inter-generational 'clash' is highlighted by the diversification strategy of earlier generations in contrast to the single business focus of the current manager.

*M H Hire*'s centralized structure and simple control system suggests this firm may be in the early phases of stage 3. In fact the entrepreneurial role is still strongly evident in this firm run by a growth oriented visionary. That being the case, the authority structure has yet to be developed to the same extent as the division of activities and this may well be the next transition for the firm to undergo. Coinciding with such changes would be the development of more sophisticated systems to supplement the current reliance on broad based information. The firm has been very successful in its growth and development but should now consolidate as it moves through stage 3.

## Stage 3 Firms Facing High Uncertainty

Another group of firms in this stage did, however, recognize high levels of uncertainty in their particular environments. This is understandable given the diversity of industries represented in the study. All these firms pursued high differentiation strategies. It is important however that such firms ensure that they have adequate and consistent controls in place.

The very large *L F Transport* has both sophisticated and broad based information systems to support a cadre of professional managers recruited in waves that seemed to coincide with development phases. Because of its size, complexity, and diversity, this firm has much in common with large public companies. The success of the firm is largely a result of the soundly based strategies for growth, implemented by the founder over the past 45 years.

Other successful firms (*C K Meats* and *A B Carr*) in this stage that encounter high levels of uncertainty with high differentiation strategies, have also developed sophisticated and broadly based information systems. In the case of *C K Meats*, these systems are sustained through a centralized management structure that probably needs to be extended through more delegation to enable it to develop further.

Less successful, however, is *M W Metals* whose centralized management is supported only by simple systems. This is due largely to some protracted problems which began when computerized systems were introduced. Furthermore, the breadth of information utilized by management in making decisions is only marginally classified as broadly based. In recent years, the managing director has suffered from the lack of professional and family support in running the business that has had to be refocussed. Interestingly, entry of the family to the particular line of business that now has become the core business was almost by chance. Family problems have also beset the firm. Some managers have held key appointments because they were family members, but were ill-suited to the demands of these positions.

## Elaboration of Structure (Stage 4) Firms

The average profile for these firms is 'more of the same'. As the stage label suggests, these firms have developed further to require more levels of decentralized management and the necessary administrative controls to support such structures. As noted earlier, relatively few family firms have reached this stage. The case of *S F Printers* is interesting because it highlights how individual firms can strategically choose atypical combinations of structures and systems and still be successful. In this case two brothers jointly manage the business through a distinct division of responsibilities and with the support of a highly professional team of managers. The level of technical sophistication employed in the business implies high degrees of decentralization will be most effective. A form of clan control seems to operate. However it is based on the professionalization of the managers rather than a sense of shared values that arise out of family. This case analysis is summarized in Table 7.5.

**Table 7.5    Life cycle patterns of case firms**

| Stage/Firm | | Uncertainty | Strategy (Differentiation) | Structure | Content of Control Systems | Form of Control Systems |
|---|---|---|---|---|---|---|
| **Stage 2** | Profile | Med. | Mod. | Cent. | Simple | Narrow |
| P B Hardware | | Med. | High | Cent. | Simple | Narrow |
| Display Services | | Med. | High | Cent. | Simple | Broad |
| | | | | | | |
| **Stage 3** | Profile | Med. | Mod. | Decent. | Sophist. | Broad |
| B F Constructions | | Med. | Low | Cent. | Simple | Narrow |
| H M Hire | | Med. | Mod. | Cent. | Simple | Broad |
| K F Foods | | Med. | Mod. | Decent. | Sophist. | Broad |
| R X Engineering | | Low | Mod. | Decent. | Sophist. | Broad |
| M W Metals | | High | High | Cent. | Simple | Broad |
| C K Meats | | High | High | Cent. | Sophist. | Broad |
| A B Carr | | High | High | Decent. | Sophist. | Broad |
| L F Transport | | High | High | Decent. | Sophist. | Broad |
| | | | | | | |
| **Stage 4** | Profile | Med. | Mod. | Decent. | Sophist. | Broad |
| S F Printers | | High | Low | Decent. | Simple | Narrow |

Learning Task 1, the need for management systems that are adequate for the firm's internal and external environment, as well as its stage of development, emerged strongly from the quantitative analysis. The remaining guidelines emerged from the more qualitative detailed case analyses. We saw that firms that learn to professionalize their management and controls tend to be those that grow and develop. Given the high interest by family firms in growth, compatible strategies, structures and systems must be developed to achieve this goal. Interestingly, the approach to professionalizing management is not the same for all cases. As the case of *S F Printers* showed, firms can be successful with some unusual combinations of structures and systems. While unusual, the elements in combination are still mutually compatible.

## Conclusion and Summary

Both the quantitative and the qualitative analyses taken together suggest that, despite the complexities and paradoxes of learning family business, there are some consistent pathways through them that can be counted on to work. As we saw from the chapters dedicated to the issues of learning business, learning *our* business, learning to lead our business, and finally, learning to let go our business, learning family business means dealing with a series of paradoxes. These paradoxes arose from the distinctive nature of family business, specifically the ways the essentially dissimilar factors of 'family' and 'business' need to be brought together. This paradoxical nature of the family business was often reiterated by our informants, who consistently felt that family businesses were somehow different and special, despite being 'just like any other business'.

The contradictions between the 'family' nature of the business and the 'business' nature of the business were enduring ones. As a result, the pathways through the paradoxes were ways of managing them, not of making them disappear.

As has emerged from our examination of the learning paradoxes in Chapters 3 to 6, however, the relationship with the business life cycle seems to become increasingly salient as learning progresses, even though the demands of learning itself become increasingly more complex. In the first learning stage, 'learning business', the learning pathway – go outside the business – is essentially independent of the business life cycle stage of the firm. However even at this stage, the business life cycle suggests how the place and the type of learning might be strategically chosen to further the aspiring CEO's understanding of the life cycle stage the family firm has reached, and how its next stage of development might be undertaken.

The salience of the business life cycle showed itself still more in the next learning stage: learning *our* business. Though the learner needed to absorb the broad philosophies and special qualities of the family business, the changes brought about by the firm's progression along the life cycle curve also pointed out how he or she needed to modify the detail of those philosophies and qualities.

The learning tasks which are involved in learning to lead the family business and, as a special part of leadership, learning to let go of the family firm, prove to be the most complex of all. In the first of these instances, the task of leadership involve making complex choices to optimize the firm's management systems in relation to aspects of its internal and external environment. Similarly, letting go the family business typically requires the creation of more formalized management development systems which will serve the business once the current CEO was no longer there. No longer is it possible for the learner to pursue a single, universal and conceptually simple pathway to manage the paradox (as with phase one 'learning business', which aspiring leaders dealt with by leaving the family business) or even to modify some existing philosophies and values (as in the second phase of learning, in which aspiring leaders learnt to 'continue differently'). In the third and fourth stages of learning, leading and, finally, letting go the family firm, the leader is faced with an array of strategic choices about the firm's response to its environment, as well as demands for its professionalization. In the fourth learning stage, learning to leave our business, the incumbent CEO must give his or her attention to these same issues in anticipation of a time when he or she will no longer be there. Moreover, the move towards professionalization needs to be merged seamlessly with the family nature of the business. No simple solutions are possible and, just as with the other paradoxes, the paradoxes cannot be made to disappear.

Yet the situation, while complex, is not random or chaotic for those aspiring to the leadership task. The business life cycle provides a mechanism for coming to grips with the diversity of approaches to these tasks of leading family firms. From our quantitative and qualitative analyses of family firms at varying stages of their life cycle, we derived five broad approaches which serve as learning tasks for the success of family business management:

- Learning Task 1: Leaders of family firms should adopt management systems which are adequate for the demands of their external and internal environments, as well as their firm's stage of development.

**Table 7.6  Learning priorities, paradoxes and pathways – linked to the organizational life cycle**

| LEARNING ... | PRIORITY | PARADOX | PATHWAYS | ORGANIZATIONAL LIFE CYCLE EFFECT |
|---|---|---|---|---|
| ... Business | Proficiency | Inside–Outside | Go outside | Minimal |
| ... *Our* business | Perpetuating values | Continuing differently | 1) Keep philosophies, not details<br>2) Learn market value of family business values | Some |
| ... To *lead* our business | Perspicacity | Informal formality | No simple pathways but address learning tasks 1 to 5 | Major |
| ... To *let go* our business | Prescience | Leading to let go | 1) Develop timeline for retirement<br>2) Create management development systems<br>3) Stick to plan | Major |

- Learning Task 2: Leaders of family firms should design an internally consistent package of strategies, structures and systems.
- Learning Task 3: Management systems must dynamically evolve as the business grows and matures.
- Learning Task 4: Professionalism in management is vital for systems development.
- Learning Task 5: Without succession plans, professionalization of the firm is seriously inhibited.

Table 7.6 shows the priorities, paradoxes and pathways for each of the learning stages, together with the effect of the business life cycle at each stage.

The five learning tasks which appear instead of simple pathways for family business leaders seem to be critical to success in the Australian family owned business. They may seem to overly emphasize the development of monitoring (control) systems, and this might appear to be counter-intuitive for family firms in which clan controls might be expected to predominate. But this is contradicted by our research as well as the empirical evidence of Schulze *et al.* (2001) concerning agency costs in family firms. Family firms which, as they approach maturity, do not introduce more formalized controls, professionalize their staff management practices, from describing job roles to creating succession plans, and instigate good governance practices which echo those of non-family firms, are likely to perform less well than family firms which do take on these tasks. The list of practices arising from the hypotheses which Schulze *et al.* (2001) tested, correspond closely to the learning tasks that our study and the early work of Moores and Mula (2000) have been shown to be vitally important for CEOs of family businesses to master. They reveal the necessity to develop monitoring systems, albeit in a phased way, driven by the firm's development in the stages of the organizational life cycle. That is, there is less need for formal systems in stages one and two of the life cycle of a firm, but management systems need to be anticipated and developed as firms grow and move to maturity. These are the key lessons that leaders of family firms need to acquire.

These learning tasks serve as a set of broad management guidelines for those family owned businesses seeking to grow and develop through the life cycle stages. Our work suggests both that CEOs of family firms who successfully negotiate the special learning paradoxes of family business, and guide their firms through the necessary life cycle transitions, can increase the firm's chances for survival and growth.

## References

Gordon, L. A. and Narayanan, V. K. (1984), 'Management accounting systems, perceived environmental uncertainty and organization structure: An empirical investigation', *Accounting, Organizations and Society*, vol. 1, pp. 33-47.

Moores, K. and Mula, J. (2000), 'The Salience of Market, Bureaucratic, and Clan Controls in the Management of Family firm Transitions: Some Tentative Australian Evidence', *Family Business Review*, vol. 13, no. 2, pp. 91-106.

Schulze, William S., Lubatkin, Michael H., Dino, Richard N. and Buchholtz, Ann K. (2001), 'Agency Relationships in Family Firms: Theory and Evidence', *Organizational Science*, vol. 12, no. 2, March-April, pp. 99-116.

# Appendix

# How We Did the Study

In the earlier chapters, we have presented summary results of our qualitative and quantitative research into Australian family businesses to show both how incumbent CEOs of family businesses passed through a series of distinct learning phases and also how their businesses have survived and grown as CEOs developed ways of coping with the pressures of their external and internal environments. Here we discuss in some detail the methodological issues which relate to the design and conduct of the research. Additionally, the details of statistical findings are reported more fully.

## Data Collection

The study collected information in two ways: a mailed questionnaire and follow-up detailed interviews with selected respondents. Firstly, data collected from questionnaires were analysed and descriptive statistics were generated. Questionnaire responses were then factor analysed, and finally the factors were correlation analysed. The statistical techniques used will be explained in some detail later.

### Quantitative Data

A six-part questionnaire provided data on key areas known to affect the success of business management: the competitive environment, strategies, structure, and control systems. Responses to questions in these areas were sought on seven-point Likert-type scales anchored at both ends to facilitate statistical analysis. Additional information was also provided concerning the ownership structure and management of the business and various identifying characteristics such as the name of the business, its industry code, principal products and legal structure. Structural measures enabled the objective identification of each firm's stage of development according to Quinn and Cameron's (1983) summary life cycle model discussed in Chapter 2.

CEOs were invited to assess the current stage of development of their family firm using an eight stage organizational life cycle scale adapted from Adizes (1979). Because our study was deliberately confined to firms which had been in existence for at least five years and which were controlled by second, or later generation family members, a set of filter questions was included early in the questionnaire. Any firms which did not fit the characteristics defined by these questions were filtered out early, and their responses to the questionnaire were not used for the study.

Relevance, brevity, simplicity and clarity of questions are important factors in any questionnaire design. Relevance and brevity are important because questionnaires that appear as if they could be answered within a very short time (that is, about 30 minutes) have been shown to have the best chance of eliciting a response (Roszkowski and Bean, 1990). A short form type of questionnaire adapted from previous studies (Khandwalla, 1972; Gordon and Narayanan, 1984; Chenhall and Morris, 1986; Miller, 1988; Miller and Friesen, 1982) was used. The questionnaire itself was produced in the form of a fourteen-page booklet.

Simplicity was achieved by requiring all responses to be made by circling the appropriate number on a seven-point scale. This reduced the likelihood of confusion on the part of the respondents, and lessened the time spent in reading instructions (Emory and Cooper, 1991). Clarity is important to make the intent of the question is clear to respondents and was assessed by pre-testing the questionnaire on a selected number of known second generation family businesses. Only minor modifications resulted from the pilot testing. It is also important to establish clarity of constructs. Often the phenomenon about which we wish to collect information cannot be measured directly. In these cases we must find a proxy measure which we believe represents the phenomenon of interest, and it is these proxy measures which we call constructs. For example, no way of directly measuring intelligence exists. Constructs, such as scores on examinations, might be used as proxies for intelligence. The extent to which the construct validly represents the phenomenon can vary, so it becomes important that constructs used are clear so that we have confidence in them.

Questionnaires were sent to the CEOs of approximately two thousand firms thought to be family owned and operated. As no official database exists for family owned businesses, the true size of this group of firms is unknown. Accordingly, our survey recipients were identified from a variety of sources including Horwath and Horwath client lists, ANZ Bank –

Queensland, *Who's Who in Australia, Business Queensland* listings; and the Dunn and Bradstreet *Key Business Directory*. In the case of the two published directories, key characteristics likely to indicate a family firm were adopted as selection criteria. These characteristics included:

- business names which included the words 'and Son(s)';
- directors, owners, and partners of the same family name.

A total of 341 firms responded. A number of firms fully completed the questionnaire even though they did not meet the test in the filter questions. A few respondents had not been in business for more than five years despite being managed by second generation family members and were subsequently excluded. What was more surprising was the number of first generation firms (about 16 per cent of respondents) who completed the questionnaire. Others excluded were those that had indicated they were not family businesses or that they were not now family businesses having been sold or gone public. 278 firms provided usable responses on which the subsequent analyses were based. About 100 of the mailed questionnaires were turned unopened. It is worthy of note that the response rate from known family firms was higher than that from the unknown list (Dunn and Bradstreet).

*Response Rate*

The filter questions made response rates less easy to ascertain and indeed less relevant. Nevertheless, given the diversity of firms and the sources from which we derived the list, we judged the response to the survey to be good.

*Qualitative Data*

Extensive interviews were conducted with chief executive officers during visits to a diverse range of family businesses throughout Australia. During these visits senior managers were invited to chronicle and reflect on both the development of the family business and how they had learned to manage it. These oral histories concentrated upon business transitions and changes and the internal and/or external factors that prompted change. They also dealt with perceived transitions in terms of the incumbent leader's own relationship with the business. Documentary evidence was obtained in the form of company reports and publications, together with newspaper articles about the business to substantiate and add detail to the oral histories and personal stories. The emphasis in these interviews was to highlight the major phases of development of the business and the learning phases discerned by incumbent CEOs. Data collected during the company visits enriched the understanding of family business management and learning issues obtained through the survey responses.

## Quantitative Analysis Techniques

Large amounts of information were collected but before any inferences could be generated, the data needed to be organized and summarized. Firstly, descriptive statistics were produced, factor analysis performed, and finally correlation analysis undertaken. Descriptive statistics involve arranging, summarizing and presenting a mass of data so the meaningful essentials can be extracted. These include calculating averages, deviations and so on about particular characteristics of the data (Zikmund, 1991).

The next step involved effectively analyzing a large volume of data through the use of data reduction techniques. For this, as mentioned briefly in Chapter 5, we used a conventional factor analysis. Factor analysis is a generic name give to a class of multivariate statistical methods whose primary purpose is data reduction and summarization. Broadly speaking, it addresses the problem of analysing the interrelationships among a number of variables (responses to questions contained in the questionnaire), and then explaining these variables in terms of their common, underlying dimensions (factors). By using factor analysis, it is possible to identify the separate dimensions being measured by the survey, and determine a factor loading for each variable (test item) on each factor.

The general purpose of factor analytic techniques is to find a way of summarizing and condensing the information contained in a number of original variables into a smaller set of new composite dimensions (factors) with a minimum loss of information (Hair *et al.*, 1987). To be meaningful, the technique calculates the percentage of variance explained by the factor, as well as tests for reliability. A good factor solution is both simple and interpretable. The SPSS statistical computer package was used where scree tests were applied to the eigen plots to extract factors which were then orthogonally rotated using varimax procedures. Finally, the derived factors were subjected to correlational techniques. Correlation is a process whereby we examine the incidence of occurrence of factors with others.

## Quantitative Results

In the next section, we present tables of descriptive statistics for five of the variables (attributes) of the research design presented in Chapter 2, that is, *Environmental Uncertainty*, *Strategies*, *Structure*, *Control Systems – Content*, and *Control Systems – Form*. (The detailed correlation results for life cycle stage were presented in Chapter 7.) We follow the descriptive statistics for each variable with a table showing its underlying dimensions as revealed by the factor analysis. After that, we present the results of both partial and correlation analysis to measure the strengths of the associations between the variables. These results were presented in Chapter 5.

### Environmental Uncertainty

A set of seven questions some with sub-parts elicited ten answers describing aspects of the firm's competitive environment. Table A.1 sets out the average results for each *Environmental Uncertainty* question, together with the standard deviation, which indicates the spread of responses across the group. The mean response was 4.56 across all questions, suggesting that incumbent CEOs of family businesses perceive a moderate degree of environmental uncertainty confronting their firms.

**Table A.1 Environmental uncertainty – descriptive statistics**

| Environment Measures | Mean | Std Deviation |
|---|---|---|
| Overall measure (PEU) | 4.56 | 1.86 |
| Intensity of external constraints | 6.1 | 1.1 |
| Price competition | 6.0 | 1.2 |
| Stability of economic environment | 4.8 | 1.6 |
| Number of new products marketed | 4.7 | 2.1 |
| Predictability of customers | 4.4 | 1.5 |
| Predictability of competitors | 4.3 | 1.7 |
| Stability of technological environment | 4.0 | 1.7 |
| Competition for inputs | 4.0 | 2.1 |
| Competition for human resources | 3.6 | 1.5 |

*Dimensions of Environmental Uncertainty*

Table A.2 shows that there were two main factors underlying *Environmental Uncertainty.* They were labelled *Technoeconomic Stability* (Cronbach alpha = 0.65) and *Competition and Constraints* (Cronbach alpha = 1.51).

**Table A.2    Dimensions of environmental uncertainty**

| **Factor 1: Technoeconomic Stability** (Reliability: 0.65) | **Loading** | **% Variance** |
|---|---|---|
| Technological stability | 0.84 | |
| Frequency of technological discoveries | 0.79 | |
| Introduction of new products | 0.59 | |
| Economic stability | 0.47 | |
| | | 25.4 |
| **Factor 2: Competition & Constraints** (Reliability: 0.51) | | |
| Intensity of price competition | 0.69 | |
| Intensity of competition for inputs | 0.66 | |
| Intensity of competition for human resources | 0.61 | |
| External constraints | 0.47 | |
| | | 13.9 |
| **Percentage of variance explained by the factors** | | 39.3 |

*Strategies*

The questionnaire included twenty-three questions covering the firm's approach to products, company expansion, marketing, the emphasis on quality, and the use of external advisers. Table A.3 presents the extent to which these various strategic approaches were employed by family owned businesses. The overall response of 3.68 suggests, as noted in Chapter 5, that family firms make only modest use of explicit strategies. However all average results need to be interpreted cautiously especially since some strategies were totally rejected by a large number of family firms. Franchising and vertical integration downwards and upwards were examples of strategies largely rejected by family firms. However family firms on average tend to favour product differentiation type strategies as opposed to cost leadership ones.

## Table A.3   Strategies

| *Strategy* Measures | Mean | Std Deviation |
|---|---|---|
| Overall measure *Strategies* | 3.68 | 2.12 |
| Importance of quality | 6.3 | 1.1 |
| Number of product lines | 5.3 | 1.9 |
| Competitors' cooperation | 4.8 | 1.9 |
| Small product modifications | 4.6 | 1.6 |
| Importance of new products | 4.7 | 1.8 |
| First to market | 4.5 | 1.7 |
| Market segmentation | 4.4 | 1.9 |
| Major product innovation | 4.3 | 1.6 |
| Prestige pricing | 4.3 | 1.9 |
| Advertising | 4.3 | 2.0 |
| Price cutting | 4.2 | 1.9 |
| Risk attitudes of managers | 4.0 | 1.4 |
| External advisers | 4.0 | 1.7 |
| Geographical expansion | 3.6 | 2.0 |
| Distribution channels | 3.4 | 2.0 |
| Technological similarities of product line | 3.1 | 1.9 |
| Lobbying government | 3.0 | 1.9 |
| Marketing strategy similarities of product line | 2.8 | 1.8 |
| Diversify internally | 2.4 | 1.6 |
| Diversify externally | 1.9 | 1.4 |
| Vertical integration – upwards | 1.8 | 1.6 |
| Vertical integration – downwards | 1.6 | 1.3 |
| Franchising | 1.4 | 1.3 |

## Dimensions of Strategies

The factor analysis of the Strategy variable revealed three underlying factors: *Product Differentiation*, *Diversification*, and *Marketing* alternatives. The dominant factor, *Product Differentiation* (Cronbach alpha

= 0.71), consisted largely of new product introductions and market segmentation. The second most important factor was *Diversification* strategies (Cronbach alpha = 0.52). The third strategy factor (Cronbach alpha = 0.45), labelled *Marketing* strategies, was relatively unreliable. Table A.4 sets out these results.

### Table A.4   Dimensions of *Strategies*

| Factor 1: Product Differentiation Strategies | Loading | % Variance |
|---|---|---|
| (Reliability: 0.71) | | |
| Importance of new products | 0.72 | |
| Market segmentation | 0.63 | |
| First to market new products | 0.58 | |
| Prestige pricing | 0.53 | |
| Distribution channels | 0.49 | |
| Advertising | 0.49 | |
| Differentiated product lines | 0.48 | |
| Importance of quality | 0.46 | |
| | | 18.1 |
| **Factor 2: Diversification Strategies** | | |
| (Reliability: 0.52) | | |
| Diversify externally | 0.61 | |
| Diversify internally | 0.59 | |
| Geographical expansion | 0.54 | |
| Vertical integration – upwards | 0.54 | |
| | | 7.6 |
| **Factor 3: Marketing Strategies** | | |
| (Reliability: 0.45) | | |
| Product innovations | 0.55 | |
| Cooperation with competitors | 0.53 | |
| Price cutting | 0.50 | |
| Risk attitudes of managers | 0.44 | |
| | | 6.0 |
| **Percentage of variance explained by 3 factors** | | 31.7 |

*Structure*

Six questions that produced ten individual answers were used to measure
the degrees of delegation, divisionalization and formalization operating in
family businesses. The overall average at 3.97 suggested modest levels of
structure exist in Australian family firms. Table A.5 presents these results.

**Table A.5** *Structure*

| Structure Measures | Mean | Std Deviation |
|---|---|---|
| Overall measure: *Strategies* | 3.97 | 2.04 |
| Product divisional structure | 5.0 | 1.9 |
| Daily decision-making level | 4.8 | 1.7 |
| Departmental structure | 4.6 | 1.9 |
| Delegation – pricing | 4.4 | 1.9 |
| Delegation – new product development | 4.0 | 1.8 |
| Divisional structure | 3.9 | 2.0 |
| Delegation – budget allocations | 3.7 | 2.0 |
| Delegation – hiring and firing managers | 3.7 | 2.3 |
| Specificity of job tasks | 3.3 | 1.7 |
| Delegation – large investments | 2.3 | 1.7 |

*Dimensions of Structure*

As with *Environmental Uncertainty*, a two-dimensional structure was found
to underlie the *Structure* variable. The delegation questions all loaded
together to produce a *Structure of Authority* factor (Cronbach alpha = 0.82).
The questions relating to the *Structure of Activities* (departments,
divisions), loaded onto another factor (Cronbach alpha = 0.60) as labelled.
Table A.6 overleaf presents these results.

*Control Systems*

As noted in Chapter 5, we assessed both the form and the content of control
systems in family firms. The nineteen *Content* questions ascertained the
extent to which a variety of largely financial controls were used in the
management of family businesses. The ten *Form* questions sought an
indication of the importance of the scope, focus, quantification, and

timeliness of information to the firm when the incumbent CEO was making decisions.

Tables A.7 and A.9 present the descriptive results for *Control Systems – Content* and *Control Systems – Form*, respectively. The overall average for all *Content* variables was 4.24, with the strongest averages being achieved by family businesses' use of computerized systems, the preparation of monthly profit and loss statements, and the control of cash by preparation of cashflow statements.

*Dimensions of Control Systems – Content*

The factor analysis of the *Control Systems – Content* questions revealed an underlying five-factor structure. The first three factors, which were also the most reliable, were labelled *Management Controls* (Cronbach alpha = 0.81), *Operational Controls* (Cronbach alpha = 0.74), and *Financial Reporting* (Cronbach alpha = 0.74). The remaining two factors, *Accounting Systems* (Cronbach alpha = 0.50) and *External Controls* were also less reliable. Only three questions loaded onto these factors. Table A.8 sets out the factor analysis results for *Control Systems – Content*.

**Table A.6   Dimensions of *Structure***

| Factor 1: Structuring of Authority | Loading | % Variance |
|---|---|---|
| (Reliability: 0.82) | | |
| Delegation – budget allocations | 0.80 | |
| Delegation – hiring | 0.79 | |
| Delegation – pricing | 0.72 | |
| Delegation – large investments | 0.73 | |
| Delegation – new products | 0.71 | |
| | | 31.3 |
| **Factor 2: Structuring of Activities** | | |
| (Reliability: 0.60) | | |
| Product divisional structure | 0.80 | |
| Departmental structure | 0.72 | |
| Divisional structure | 0.64 | |
| | | 16.2 |
| **Percentage of variance explained by the factors** | | 47.5 |

## Table A.7   *Control Systems – Content*

| Control Systems – Content Measures | Mean | Std Deviation |
|---|---|---|
| Overall measure: *Control Systems – Content* | 4.24 | 2.27 |
| Computerized systems | 6.1 | 1.6 |
| Monthly profit and loss | 5.8 | 1.8 |
| Cashflow statements | 5.5 | 1.9 |
| Standard costs | 5.0 | 2.1 |
| Monthly balance sheet | 4.9 | 2.3 |
| Participation in budgeting | 4.6 | 2.1 |
| Cost centres | 4.3 | 2.2 |
| Operational controls | 4.1 | 2.2 |
| Profit centres | 4.1 | 2.3 |
| Long term planning | 4.0 | 2.1 |
| Frequency of formal directors meetings | 3.9 | 1.9 |
| Performance evaluation | 3.9 | 2.1 |
| External auditing | 3.7 | 2.3 |
| Internal rate of return | 3.6 | 2.1 |
| Comparison with industry averages | 3.5 | 2.0 |
| Internal auditing | 3.5 | 2.2 |
| TQM | 3.4 | 2.2 |
| Manual systems | 2.6 | 1.9 |

## Control Systems – Form

The average for *Control Systems – Form* questions was 4.8, with all responses being skewed towards the higher end of the scale. This indicates the importance to family businesses of the timely delivery of a diverse range of information.

The ten Form questions coalesced into two reliable factors: *Scope of Information* (Cronbach alpha = 0.72) and *Timeliness of Information* (Cronbach alpha = 0.67). Table A.10 presents the factor analysis for *Control Systems – Form.*

## Table A.8 Dimensions of *Control Systems – Content*

| Factor 1: Management Controls | Loading | % Variance |
|---|---|---|
| (Reliability: 0.81) | | |
| Profit centres | 0.82 | |
| Cost centres | 0.75 | |
| Performance evaluation | 0.72 | |
| Participation in budgeting | 0.62 | |
| Industry averages | 0.53 | |
| Long term planning | 0.49 | |
| | | 31.8 |
| **Factor 2: Operational Controls** | | |
| (Reliability: 0.74) | | |
| Operations control techniques | 0.77 | |
| TQM techniques | 0.67 | |
| Internal rates of return (IRR) | 0.65 | |
| Internal auditing | 0.57 | |
| Standard costs | 0.57 | |
| | | 9.0 |
| **Factor 3: Financial Reporting** | | |
| (Reliability: 0.74) | | |
| Monthly balance sheets | 0.88 | |
| Monthly profit and loss statements | 0.85 | |
| Cashflow statements | 0.48 | |
| | | 7.8 |
| **Factor 4: Accounting Systems** | | |
| (Reliability: 0.50) | | |
| Manual systems | 0.80 | |
| Computerized systems | 0.69 | |
| | | 6.46 |
| **Factor 5: External Controls** | | |
| External auditing | 0.83 | |
| | | 5.7 |
| **Percentage of variance explained by the factors** | | 60.8 |

**Table A.9**  *Control Systems – Form*

| Control Systems – Form Measures | Mean | Std Deviation |
|---|---|---|
| Overall measure Control Systems – Form | 4.80 | 1.76 |
| Time between event and receiving information | 5.8 | 1.3 |
| Frequency of reports | 5.3 | 1.7 |
| Non-economic data | 5.1 | 1.6 |
| Delays if reporting information | 4.9 | 1.3 |
| External statistical data | 4.9 | 1.7 |
| Historical data related to future | 4.7 | 1.8 |
| Information supplied automatically | 4.5 | 1.7 |
| Non-financial data – market | 4.4 | 1.8 |
| Quantification of future events | 4.4 | 2.0 |
| Non-financial data – product | 4.1 | 2.0 |

**Table A.10  Dimensions of *Control Systems – Form***

| Factor 1: Scope of Information | Loading | % Variance |
|---|---|---|
| (Reliability: 0.72) | | |
| Historical data related to future | 0.71 | |
| Quantification of future events | 0.68 | |
| Non-financial market information | 0.63 | |
| Non-economic information | 0.62 | |
| External statistical information | 0.59 | |
| Non-financial product information | 0.54 | |
| | | 32.5 |
| **Factor 2: Timeliness of Information** | | |
| (Reliability: 0.67) | | |
| Delays in reporting information | 0.77 | |
| Information supplied automatically | 0.76 | |
| Frequency of reports | 0.71 | |
| Delay between event occurring and receiving information | 0.61 | |
| | | 14.8 |
| **Percentage of variance explained by 2 factors** | | 47.3 |

## Table A.11  Correlation matrix

| | Environmental Uncertainty | | Structure | | Strategies | | |
| --- | --- | --- | --- | --- | --- | --- | --- |
| | techno-economic | competition & constraints | of authority | of activities | differentiation | diversification | marketing |
| *Environmental Uncertainty* | | | | | | | |
| ▪ techno-economic | | | | | | | |
| ▪ competition & constraints | 0.000 | | | | | | |
| *Structure* | | | | | | | |
| ▪ of authority | 0.001 | 0.077 | | | | | |
| ▪ of activities | 0.166 | 0.075 | 0.000 | | | | |
| *Strategies* | | | | | | | |
| ▪ differentiation | 0.394 | 0.017 | 0.118 | 0.197 | | | |
| ▪ diversification | 0.031 | -0.074 | 0.161 | 0.133 | 0.000 | | |
| ▪ marketing | 0.311 | 0.111 | -0.060 | 0.134 | 0.000 | 0.000 | |
| *Control Systems – Content* | | | | | | | |
| ▪ management controls | 0.076 | 0.076 | 0.295 | 0.275 | 0.198 | 0.245 | 0.068 |
| ▪ operational controls | 0.106 | 0.060 | 0.146 | 0.228 | 0.137 | 0.101 | 0.146 |
| ▪ financial reporting | 0.030 | 0.104 | 0.077 | 0.172 | 0.039 | 0.136 | 0.059 |
| ▪ accounting systems | 0.143 | 0.057 | 0.149 | 0.087 | 0.089 | 0.023 | 0.084 |
| ▪ external controls | 0.015 | 0.036 | 0.054 | 0.063 | 0.069 | 0.051 | 0.081 |
| *Control Systems – Form* | | | | | | | |
| ▪ scope of information | 0.124 | 0.109 | 0.191 | 0.220 | 0.367 | 0.122 | 0.065 |
| ▪ timeliness of information | 0.138 | 0.045 | 0.130 | 0.162 | 0.083 | 0.042 | 0.079 |

## Correlation Analysis

The relationships between the elements in this reduced set of dimensions were examined through a series of correlation analyses based on the saved factor scores. A two-stage approach was used. First, simple Pearson correlations among the factors underlying all the research attributes: *Environmental Uncertainty, Structure, Strategy, Control Systems – Content* and *Control Systems – Form,* were computed. Second, partial correlations among the variables taken two at a time and controlling for all others were determined. The reason for this approach was to see if one of the variables was the driving force in the simple first order correlations.

Bivariate correlation provides a single number which summarizes a relationship between two variables. These correlation coefficients (r) indicate the degree to which the variation or change in one variable is related to variation of change in another.

**Table A.11  Correlation matrix (continued)**

| | | Control Systems – Content | | | | | Control Systems – Form | |
|---|---|---|---|---|---|---|---|---|
| | management controls | operational control | financial reporting | accounting systems | external controls | scope of information | timeliness of information |
| *Control Systems – Content* | | | | | | | |
| ▪ management controls | | | | | | | |
| ▪ operational controls | 0.000 | | | | | | |
| ▪ financial reporting | 0.000 | 0.000 | | | | | |
| ▪ accounting systems | 0.000 | 0.000 | 0.000 | | | | |
| ▪ external controls | 0.000 | 0.000 | 0.000 | 0.000 | | | |
| *Control Systems – Form* | | | | | | | |
| ▪ scope of information | 0.371 | 0.362 | 0.136 | -0.074 | -0.107 | | |
| ▪ timeliness of information | 0.191 | 0.024 | 0.084 | 0.121 | 0.024 | 0.000 | |

Level of significance:  @ < 1%   @ < 5%

Note: The zero correlation between factors within the same construct (for example, *Technoeconomic Uncertainty – Competition and Constraints*) arises because of the orthogonal rotation used in factor analysis extraction procedures.

## Table A.12  Partial correlation analysis

| | Environmental Uncertainty | | Structure | | Strategies | | |
|---|---|---|---|---|---|---|---|
| | techno-economic | competition and constraints | of authority | of activities | differentiation | diversification | marketing |
| **Control Systems – Content** | | | | | | | |
| ▪ management controls | -0.035 | 0.052 | 0.260 | 0.248 | 0.045 | 0.208 | 0.092 |
| ▪ operational controls | -0.011 | 0.023 | 0.149 | 0.205 | -0.011 | 0.096 | 0.138 |
| ▪ financial reporting | -0.074 | 0.093 | 0.092 | 0.176 | 0.005 | 0.142 | 0.076 |
| ▪ accounting systems | 0.095 | 0.052 | 0.183 | 0.097 | 0.063 | 0.023 | 0.055 |
| ▪ external controls | 0.028 | 0.058 | 0.056 | 0.081 | -0.043 | 0.044 | -0.096 |
| **Control Systems – Form** | | | | | | | |
| ▪ scope of information | -0.017 | 0.065 | 0.041 | 0.001 | 0.290 | -0.007 | -0.027 |
| ▪ timeliness of information | 0.081 | -0.011 | 0.062 | 0.069 | 0.021 | -0.077 | 0.006 |

Level of significance: @ < 1%　　@ < 5%　　@ < 10%

A correlation coefficient not only summarizes the strength of association between a pair of variables, but also provides an easy means for comparing the strength of relationship between one pair of variables and a different pair. Table A.11 presents the results of the simple correlation analysis and Table A.12 presents the results of the partial correlation analysis.

*Reading the Tables*

The dimensions which were correlated and the relative strength (or significance) of their correlations are indicated in the highlighted cells in each table. Cells with broken borders indicate a slight correlation between the two dimensions, that is, that there was a less than ten per cent chance that the relationship could have occurred by chance. Cells with a single border indicate a moderately significant correlation between the two dimensions, that is, that there is a less than five per cent chance that the relationship between them could have appeared by chance. Cells with a double border indicate a very strong or highly significant correlation between the dimensions, that is, that there was a less than one per cent chance that the relationship could have appeared by chance.

*Simple Correlations*

From the correlations reported in Table A.11, it is clear that, of the *Environmental Uncertainty* variables, only one, the *Technoeconomic* factor, is associated with either the content or form of the control systems. It is related to *Accounting Systems* [r = 0.143, p < 0.05] and both *Form* characteristics: (*Scope* [r = 0.124, p < 0.05] and *Timeliness* [r = 0.138, p < 0.05]. However both structural and strategic factors are significantly associated with the major content and form dimensions of control systems. Both the *Structure of Authority* [r = 0.295, p < 0.01] and the *Structure of Activities* [r = 0.275, p < 0.01] have highly significant associations with *Management Controls.*

*Operational Controls* are also positively related to these two structural factors [r = 0.146, p < 0.05; r = 0.228, p < 0.01].

Two of the strategic factors are also associated with increased levels of sophistication in *Management Controls,* as shown by the positive correlation of *Product Differentiation* [r = 0.198, p < 0.01] and *Diversification* strategies [r = 0.245, p < 0.01] with this factor.

Both the structural factors are significantly positively associated with the two form dimensions of control information. The *Structuring of Authority* and *Structuring of Activities* are positively associated with the *Scope of Information* [r = 0.191, p < 0.05; r = 0.220, p < 0.05, respectively] and the *Timeliness of Information* [r = 0.130, p < 0.05; r = 0.162, p < 0.01, respectively].

There were also some other factors than those pertaining to control systems that were related. *Technoeconomic Uncertainty* arising from technological discoveries and the economic change caused by the introduction of new products was associated with *Product Differentiation* [r = 0.394, p < 0.01] and *Marketing Strategies* [r = 0.166, p < 0.01]. The *Competition and Constraints* factor was not significantly associated with any strategic, structural or systems factors.

The implications of these results, particularly the finding that firm structures and strategies are more strongly positively associated with the characteristics of the control systems of family firms than with external uncertainties, are discussed more fully in Chapter 5.

*Partial Correlations*

As noted earlier, we used partial correlation analysis to determine if any one of the variables were driving any of the correlations found in the simple analysis. Specifically, the variables were taken two at a time controlling for all others.

The partial correlations showed that, by far, it is *Management Controls* and *Operational Controls* of family firms that are most strongly associated with both the content and the form of controls. Both the *Structuring of Authority* [r = 0.260, p < 0.01] and *Activities* [r = 0.248, p < 0.01] along with the pursuit of *Diversification Strategies* [r = 0.208, p < 0.01] are all highly positively associated with the development of sophisticated management controls. However, *Operational Controls* are not driven by *Diversification Strategies* but rather, although to a lesser extent, by *Marketing Strategies* [r = 0.138, p < 0.05]. The *Authority Structures* [r = 0.149, p < 0.01] and the *Structuring of Activities* [r = 0.205, p < 0.01] both significantly drive *Operational Controls.*

The sophistication of *Financial Reporting* tends to be driven by *Structuring of Activities* [r = 0.176, p < 0.01] and *Diversification Strategies* [r = 0.142, p < 0.05]. It is driven to a far lesser extent by the level of *Competition and Constraints* [r = 0.093, p < 0.10] prevailing in the external environment and the internal *Structuring of Authority* [r = 0.092, p < 0.10]. The development of computerized accounting systems is, interestingly, driven largely by an internal feature, the *Structuring of Authority* [r = 0.092, p < 0.10]. Lesser drivers for such systems include internal *Structuring of Activities* [r = 0.097, p < 0.10] and external *Technoeconomic Uncertainty* [r = 0.095, p < 0.10].

Concerning the form of information supplied, it is only *a Product Differentiation* strategy that drives the increasing breadth of *Scope of Information* [r = 0.290, p < 0.01]. Family firms which pursue product differentiation strategies would appear to value broad historical information external to the firm such as economic conditions, population growth and technological developments, together with other non-economic information especially if it relates to possible future events.

The partial correlation analysis tends to confirm that firm structures and strategies do drive the sophistication of controls employed by family firms. These factors impact most heavily on the *Management Controls* and *Operational Controls* used.

*Life Cycle Influences on Family Firm Management and Control*

Table A.13 below presents the detailed quantitative results for the factors of *Environmental Uncertainty, Structure, Strategies, Control Systems – Content* and *Control Systems – Form*, for a sub-set of firms in our sample which represent Stages 2, 3 and 4 of the business life cycle.

**Table A.13  Life cycle patterns of firm characteristics**

| Characteristics | Collectivity (Stage 2) Mean | Formalization and Control (Stage 3) Mean | Elaboration of Structure (Stage 4) Mean |
|---|---|---|---|
| *Environmental Uncertainty* | | | |
| ▪ technoeconomic | 3.91 | **4.57** | 4.26 |
| ▪ competition and constraints | 4.34 | **4.97** | 4.59 |
| *Structure* | | | |
| ▪ of authority | 4.31 | 4.71 | **4.91** |
| ▪ of activities | 1.99 | **2.57** | 2.11 |
| *Strategies* | | | |
| ▪ differentiation | 4.09 | 4.35 | **4.50** |
| ▪ diversification | 3.03 | **3.76** | 3.59 |
| ▪ marketing | 2.12 | 4.79 | **6.82** |
| *Control Systems – Content* | | | |
| ▪ management controls | 3.14 | 4.24 | **4.39** |
| ▪ operational controls | 3.27 | **4.01** | 3.86 |
| ▪ financial reporting | 4.72 | 5.43 | **6.39** |
| ▪ accounting systems | 4.15 | 4.35 | **4.45** |
| ▪ external controls | 3.23 | 3.72 | **4.09** |
| *Control Systems – Form* | | | |
| ▪ scope of information | 4.12 | 4.66 | **5.08** |
| ▪ timeliness of information | 4.70 | 5.15 | **5.42** |

A figure in **bold** is the largest mean for the factor measured on a scale of 1 to 7.

While family firms at all stages perceive moderate levels of environmental uncertainty, CEOs of Stage 3 firms report the most, perhaps because they are slightly more diversified. The pattern of average firm responses to this uncertainty in terms of their structure, strategies, and the content and form of their control systems, makes it clear that successful family firms develop increasingly sophisticated systems as they progress towards the *Elaboration of Structure* (Stage 4) phase of the business life cycle.

# References

Adizes, I. (1979), 'Organizational Passages: Diagnosing and Treating Lifecycle Problems of Organizations', *Organizational Dynamics*, vol. 8, no. 1, pp. 2-25.

Chenhall, R. H. and Morris, D. (1986), 'The Impact of Structure, Environment, and Interdependence on the Perceived Usefulness of Management Accounting Systems', *The Accounting Review*, vol. 56, no. 1, pp. 16-35.

Emory, C. William and Cooper, Donald R. (1991), *Business Research Methods*, 4th ed. Homewood, Il., Irwin.

Gordon, L. A. and Narayanan, V. K. (1984), 'Management accounting systems, perceived environmental uncertainty and organization structure: An empirical investigation', *Accounting, Organizations and Society*, vol. 1, pp. 33-47.

Hair, Joseph F. Jr., Anderson, Rolph E., and Tatham, Ronald L. (1987), *Multivariate Data Analysis with Readings*, 2nd ed., Tulsa, Petroleum Publishing Company.

Khandwalla, P. N. (1972), 'The Effect of Different Types of Competition on the Use of Management Controls', *Journal of Accounting Research*, pp. 275-85.

Miller, D. (1988), 'Relating Porter's business strategies to environment and structure: Analysis and performance implications,' *Academy of Management Journal*, vol. 31, no. 2, pp. 280-308.

Miller, D. and Friesen, P. H. (1982), 'Structural Change and Performance: Quantum versus Piecemeal-Incremental Approaches', *Academy of Management Journal*, pp. 867-92.

Quinn, R. E. and Cameron, K. (1983), 'Organizational life cycles and shifting criteria of effectiveness: Some preliminary evidence', *Management Science*, vol. 29, no. 1, pp. 33-51.

Roszkowski, M. J. and Bean, A. G. (1990), 'Believe It or Not! Longer Questionnaires Have Lower Response Rates', *Journal of Business and Psychology*, vol. 4, no. 4, pp. 495-509.

Zikmund, William G. (1991), *Business Research Methods*, 3rd ed., Chicago, Dryden Press.

# Index

accounting performance measures, *see*
    control(s): accounting
actual costing 20
administrivism 117
adolescence (stage of organizational life
    cycle) 16, 20, 23, 52
advertising 95, 157-8
advisers 94, 156-7
agency
    costs 31-2, 75, 102, 148
    theory 31, 102
ambassador (retirement role) 122-3, 129
appraisal systems *see* performance
    management systems
aristocratic (stage of organizational life
    cycle) 16, 21
asset acquisitions 97
auditing firms 96
Australian Bureau of Statistics (ABS)
    5-7, 10
Australian Centre for Family Business
    xi, 2
autocratic (leadership style) 87, 89

balance sheet 17, 70, 96-7, 161-2
board 6, 8, 17, 57, 79, 90, 107-13, 123,
    125, 127-8
bonuses 79, 106
budget *see* controls, budgetary
bureaucracy (stage of organizational life
    cycle) 16, 18, 21
business (definition of) 5
business life cycle see organizational life
    cycle
Business Longitudinal Survey 5-7, 10,
Business Review Weekly 1-2, 4,

Canadian Association of Family
    Enterprises 4
career path
    planning 54-5, 57, 60-61, 79, 128
    and women 54-6, 61
cashflow
    analysis 20, 66

statements 96, 97, 106, 160-2
centralization
    of power 26-7, 78, 106
    of structure 26, 54, 78, 133-4, 137,
        142-3
CEO
    as catalyst for change 87, 128
    as hero 120-4
collectivity (stage of organizational life
    cycle) 22-3, 103, 132-40, 169
communication 22, 44, 65, 76
competition 50, 93-4, 101, 135-6, 142,
    155
    and constraints 100-101, 133, 135-6,
        156, 164-9
competitors 14, 44, 50, 61, 74, 93, 95,
    105, 155, 157-8
computerized systems 96, 101, 106, 137,
    143, 160-62, 168
consumer organizations 100
context (business) 13, 23-4, 28, 32-3, 53,
    86, 91-2, 103, 112, 131, 135, 141
contingencies 13, 25, 33, 93, 111
contingency perspectives 22-5, 92
continuity (value of) 59-60, 63, 80, 82
control(s)
    accounting 20, 25, 28
    action 28
    administrative 20, 27, 141, 143
    balance of 28, 111
    behaviour 28
    budgetary 17, 20, 24-6, 43, 96-100,
        137, 159, 160-62
    bureaucratic 20, 27, 102-3, 106, 117,
        137
    clan 27, 31, 91, 102-7, 111-12, 131,
        137-8, 140, 144, 148
    classifications of 27-8
    consistency of 28-9, 99, 135-43, 148
    and cultural values ix, 27-9, 82, 88,
        91
    formal and informal 15-17, 21, 25-9,
        83, 91, 95-6, 100-112, 128,
        131, 134, 137-41, 146-8, 159